BEYOND NICE

BEYOND NICE
The Spiritual Wisdom of Adolescent Girls

Patricia H. Davis

FORTRESS PRESS / MINNEAPOLIS

BEYOND NICE
The Spiritual Wisdom of Adolescent Girls

Scripture quotations from the New Revised Standard Version of the Bible are copyright © 1989 by the Division of Christian Education of the National Council of the Churches of Christ in the United States of America and are used by permission.

Cover image: Study for "The Lady of Shalott," John William Waterhouse. Oil on canvas, c. 1894. Falmouth Art Gallery, Cornwall. Used by permission.

Lyrics (chapter 4 epigraph): "Imperfectly," Ani DiFranco. © 1992 Righteous Babe Music. All rights reserved. Used by permission.

Cover and book design: Ann Delgehausen

Library of Congress Cataloging-in-Publication Data
Davis, Patricia H.
    Beyond nice : the spiritual wisdom of adolescent girls / Patricia H. Davis.
        p. cm.
    Includes bibliographical references and index.
    ISBN 0-8006-3256-7 (alk. paper)
        1. Teenage girls—Religious life—United States. 2. Spiritual life—Christianity. I. Title.

BV4551.2 .D38 2000
277.3'0829'08352—dc21   00-040484

The paper used in this publication meets the minimum requirements of American National Standard for Information Sciences—Permanence of Paper for Printed Library Materials, ANSI Z329.48-1984.

Manufactured in the U.S.A.   AF 1-3256
05   04   03   02   01   1   2   3   4   5   6   7   8   9   10

To Margaret and Bill Davis
who taught me to love questions

Contents

Preface

"Nice girls" are always calm, controlled, quiet . . . they never
cause a ruckus, are never noisy, bossy, or aggressive, are not
anxious and do not cause trouble.
                    —"A Cultural Model of Perfection
                              for Adolescent Girls"[1]

Niceness is the opposite of spirituality. Niceness is, in fact,
the opposite of what is required to build any genuine relationship—with God or with others. While niceness can smooth
superficial human interactions, it is devastating to true intimacy.

Niceness requires putting away genuine feelings, avoiding
conflict, swallowing hurts, denying pain, and being untruthful.
Niceness requires self-denial and often self-forgetting. The nice
person eventually forgets to notice how she really feels, even in
extreme circumstances. The truly nice person doesn't even
know when she's angry, and wouldn't admit to being angry if
questioned. The nice person would never fight on her own be-
half. Most often, nice people are not able to feel strong positive
emotions either. Nice people are "calm, controlled, quiet."

Niceness is the opposite of what adults should be teaching
adolescents. Yet it is a prime virtue taught to adolescent girls
by mothers, teachers, and other adults who have internalized
dominant cultural messages about "good" women: that they

are self-sacrificing, nurturing, and never angry—that they are ultimately responsible for maintaining and protecting relationships. Girls, in fact, are taught to understand themselves in terms of the relationships of which they are a part. They learn that conflict (not-niceness) is a threat to relationships and selves, rather than that anger and other so-called negative feelings are natural human emotions that can be symptoms of relational problems.

Just at the time in their lives when girls are coming to know themselves as adults, just at the time when their awareness of what it means to be women is formed, they are often taught to be "nice" instead of to understand and deal with the complexity of adult emotional life. This usually means putting away their most important and real feelings, in favor of the kind of smiles and congeniality that will more likely win adult (and peer) approval.

True spirituality is about intimacy with God and others. This book is based in the testimony of over one hundred girls about their developing spiritualities within the context of a culture of niceness. Most of the girls in this study were very nice to me, the interviewer, but many also were courageous enough to break through niceness and to speak from their hearts about God, their families, their churches, their friends, and their relationships.

It is encouraging that most of these girls seem to see how expectations of niceness can be dangerous for them and for the development of real intimate relationships. But they also talk about the struggle to act in ways that are congruent with their true feelings when those feelings are negative or even just intense. More importantly for the adults in their lives, they talk about their need for models—especially for women—who will embody a spirituality and style of relating to others that reveals integrity between true emotions and actions. They talk about wanting and needing families and church communities that will expect them to live honestly instead of nicely. They talk about needing to be able to ask questions that are hard and challenging, and to be heard and answered. They talk about the hard areas of their own lives, their experiences (first- or second-hand) of violence and their developing sexualities. They talk about their experiences of financial and material need, and their expectations for the future.

I began this study with the idea that working with girls in a spiritual context would mean, first of all, helping girls to see the value in spirituality. I was surprised to find that most of the girls to whom I listened are already vitally interested in having a real relationship with God. And they are interested in worship, doctrine, and especially the ethical teaching of the church. *But* they wonder why adults do not address their issues of vital concern such as violence, financial problems, and sexuality. They wonder why, even when they risk asking the questions, they are ignored or given answers that are too easy. This book can be read as a plea from the girls to the adults in their lives and to the church to drop the niceness code—to listen to their sometimes difficult voices—and to move toward real relationships with them. It can also be read as an offering of gratitude for the times they have been heard and appreciated even when they weren't being nice. I am deeply indebted to these girls for their courage and willingness to talk with me. Their thoughtfulness and honesty are an inspiration to me, and I hope they will be so for others as well.

I am also indebted to many others who made this study possible: to Dean Robin Lovin and Perkins School of Theology, Southern Methodist University, for providing fellowships and time to travel and write; to Dr. Robert Armstrong and the Sam Taylor Fellowship Fund for the initial grant for the project; to Dr. James Lewis and the Louisville Institute for a summer stipend to conduct interviews about girls and worship; and to the Association of Theological Schools, Henry Luce III Fellows in Theology program for the fellowship which allowed completion of the final research and writing of the manuscript.

Thanks to others who have helped in many ways, including introducing me to the girls and allowing me to interview them in their churches and schools: Daniel Kincaid introduced me to girls at the Groton School; Headmaster William Clarkson allowed me to interview girls at the Westminster Schools in Atlanta, Georgia; Christie Shdeed arranged for me to interview students at the Parish Day School in Dallas, Texas; Professor Millie Feske introduced me to girls at St. Joseph's University in Philadelphia, Pennsylvania; Larry Cox and Kathleen Baskin introduced me to girls in Dallas, Texas; Tom and Terri Davis helped in Athens, Georgia; Susan and Jacqueline Petro helped in Atlanta, Georgia; Barbara Davis helped in Colorado. Professor Jeff introduced me to girls at Christ for the Nations College in Dallas, Texas; Bill and Peg Davis helped in Indianapolis, Indiana (and thanks, Mom, for reading an early manuscript); Sarah Megan Howery introduced me to some wonderful women's music, the lyrics of which serve as epigraphs for chapter 4; Elizabeth Gretz and Carol Adams were great encouragers and coaches; and Donna Yari helped with research on spirituality. Thanks to Michael West at Fortress for being such an astute (and humorous) guide through the publishing process.

I have much gratitude to the following churches for introducing me to girls and their parents: Westview Presbyterian and First United Methodist Churches of Longmont, Colorado; Montview Boulevard Presbyterian Church in Denver, Colorado; Church of the Crossing, Indianapolis, Indiana; Nuevo Esperanza and Greenland Hills United Methodist Churches in Dallas, Texas; First Presbyterian Church in Richardson, Texas; and Crest-Moore King United Methodist Church in Oak Cliff, Texas.

Finally, many thanks to my husband, Steve Howery, and my son, Tom—who lived with me through all the travels, tapes, transcripts, folders, writing, deadlines, etc. Your love, patience, and encouragement got me through my part of this effort!

Introduction

It was the Sunday after Christmas, and I was substitute teaching the junior high's Sunday school class. Expectations were low. When I arrived two boys were sprawled out on the couches, eyes closed, catching a few more moments of sleep before class. As I pulled some chairs into the circle next to the couches, two girls wandered in. The regular group was diminished by about half. The girls lit the gathering candle, and I joined them in saying the opening prayer.

The lesson was Jesus' great commandment: Love your neighbor as yourself. The challenge: Jesus seems to be taking for granted that we love ourselves. How do we know that we love ourselves?

One of the boys offered: "I know I love myself when our football team wins a game, and I feel really good." The second boy: "I know I love myself when my grades go up instead of down." The girls shifted uneasily in their chairs. The first, an honor student and soccer player, looked at the floor. "I know I love myself, because after I had a fight with my mother, and she left me alone, I didn't kill myself." The second girl, her best friend, agreed: "Yeah, I had a fight with my parents last week, and I didn't even hurt myself."

* * *

This incident captures broader truths about girls' religious lives—truths about relationships, self-image, and their spiritualities. These girls understand the connections between self-love and survival, between disrupted relationships and the threat of self-destruction and annihilation. For them, self-love is not about achievement or public recognition; it is essentially bound up in the ways they are able to stay in relationship with those they love. They recognize their own self-love in Jesus' command to love by their own willingness to stay alive even when important relationships are threatened. These girls' seemingly offhand comments, spoken quietly during a drowsy Sunday school hour, illustrate the necessity of listening carefully to girls, learning about their lives and their visions of themselves and the ways in which their spiritualities function as they mature into young adults. In truth, their spiritualities have been developing since early infancy.

A baby, who knows nothing of God cognitively, nevertheless has experiences of the divine. The way she is cared for by her parents; the ways she is received into her larger family of siblings, grandparents, uncles, aunts, and cousins; the ways the family's faith community introduces her to the traditions and culture of the group—all of these contribute to her developing relationship with God. The years of infancy are, in fact, the foundation of religious experience. This is the time when a child will come to know whether the universe is a good and trustworthy place, whether she is welcome in the world, and whether she will be cared for and protected by "her" people.[1]

As a girl grows into childhood, she experiences God in her family's continuing care, in her beginning prayers and religious lessons, in her connections with nature, in her relationships with friends and community members, and in the wonder and excitement of religious celebrations. Stories of God's love and goodness become important and are both comforting and challenging.

A girl realizes she is becoming a woman—ready or not—when her body and her relationships begin to change. She may begin to see (with horror or relief) that her breasts are noticeable when she wears certain shirts or blouses. She begins her monthly periods. Adults admire her in new ways, and she starts to be called a "young lady." Boys begin to treat her differently and to expect her to act differently in response to them. Her father may stop hugging her so tightly, and may even look away when she wears her bathing suit.

The main psychological developmental task of an adolescent girl is to solidify a sense of who she is, now that she is no longer a child.[2] In adolescence many girls begin to test themselves as individuals and as emerging adults—in relationships, in social activities, and in new ways of thinking. Relationships above all tell a girl who she is and what her life is about.

If a girl has been fortunate, most of her important relationships remained healthy and stable throughout childhood. Her parents loved each other and remained together. Grandparents stayed healthy and emotionally close and supportive. Cherished pets survived. Friendships matured as she did. Her community of faith welcomed her and felt to her like another kind of safe larger family. In addition, she and her family lived a satisfying life in their larger society, with enough economic resources and possibilities to live comfortably and safely. In the best circumstances, her family and friends are excited about the woman she is becoming. Religion has been a stable, loving, and protective force in her life, and she has established a warm relationship with God.

Healthy spirituality, for an adolescent girl, involves relationships that affirm who she is becoming. A girl's spirituality emanates from her *relationship with God—the one she hopes will listen to her, value her, guide her, encourage her, and protect her.* In addition, her spirituality reflects all the other important relationships in her life. Each girl's spirituality is complex and unique. It can draw her to truth and freedom, and it can help her to resist evil and oppression.

However, in North American culture girls are often at risk. Very few girls grow up in ideal emotional situations. Much very good research has been conducted on the social location of girls in this culture, showing the oppression inherent in girls' lives in terms of opportunities withheld, harassment condoned, voices silenced, and self-esteem undermined.[3] Girls are at risk for sexual and physical abuse. They are at risk for developing eating disorders; they are at risk for depression and suicide; they are at risk for deadly sexually transmitted diseases and unplanned pregnancy; they are at risk for alcohol and drug abuse; and, perhaps most importantly, they are at risk for losing a sense of their own power, value, and importance in the universe.[4]

Many girls have deep spiritual questions that arise out of these kinds of negative experiences. By adolescence most girls' images of God begin to change and deepen. They can begin to reflect upon what they have been taught—to dig deeper and to refine their spiritualities. They hope to be listened to, and they want answers to questions. They are especially frustrated that God does not often seem to answer them when they pray. They wonder if God listens; they often wonder if God cares about them. They also wonder what God expects from them, and why it isn't communicated clearly. They are very troubled about God's seeming tolerance of evil and violence.

If God seems to stand by as they are being oppressed, girls come to believe that God doesn't care about them or that God is evil. Sometimes spiritual disturbance arises out of the world itself and the often brutal reality of living in this time. Troubled girls demonstrate that even as spirituality can contribute to a positive sense of self and an appreciation of life and the cosmos, it can also contribute to depression, anxiety, and feelings of worthlessness. In the worst cases, girls' spiritualities are confusing, humiliating, and even horrifying.

* * *

In this volume, we attempt to hear girls' spiritual voices, listening intently to what girls today are telling us about themselves, their situations and relationships, and God. The volume is based on a four-year research project, which had three major goals: (1) to discover ways in which spirituality, a topic under-represented in other research on girls, positively shapes the ways girls understand themselves and their world; (2) to see if and how spirituality functions in girls' everyday lives as a part of their strategies for survival in often hostile cultures; and (3) to see if and how spirituality can also contribute to *unhealthy* attitudes, beliefs, and actions.

Some of the girls who participated in this study had very strong, positive spiritualities. They had begun to learn to relate to God in mature ways, tolerating ambiguities and paradoxes—even making sense of silence. For these girls, their spiritualities were beginning to give them a positive sense of identity and life's meaning.

Most girls who participated, however, also revealed ways in which their spiritualities were troubled. For some, the disturbance came from other unhealthy relationships. Girls whose families do not instill in them a sense that they are cherished, girls who are abused, and girls who are not taken seriously often revealed troubled relationships to God. Girls whose family religion is judgmental, harsh, and punitive often incorporated these feelings into their own relationships with God.

The methodological premise of this research was that to understand girls' spirituality it is necessary to talk and listen to *them*.[5] For this purpose I designed a questionnaire and interview format that were used to gather information and to facilitate discussion—in churches, community agencies, and schools—with girls who would agree to talk with me.[6]

The interviewing process took place in three phases. The first was an exploration of girls' God-images and how they function in girls' psychological and spiritual development. The second phase centered on girls' ways of worshiping—ways they found most meaningful and ways that were not meaningful or were even harmful to them. The third phase centered on girls' relationships to their faith communities: What kinds of communities seemed to nurture them? What aspects were less helpful? To whom in their communities would they turn for counsel and nurture? Who, if anyone, modeled the spiritual life for them? A fourth issue became clear as the interview process progressed: the ways girls were able, or not, to employ their spiritualities in dealing with experiences of violence in their families and social worlds.

Because the research method used in this study is qualitative (concerned with seeking meaning in the experiences of individuals) and not quantitative (concerned with statistical validity or replicability), the findings I present in this volume are not generalizable. In other words, this research is only really about the girls I interviewed and is not generally applicable to *all* adolescent girls. For instance, none of the girls I interviewed risked telling me about their experiences as lesbian or bisexual young women. This is understandable in our current antihomosexual culture, but a regrettable lack in this study. It is also important to note that except for several of the girls who identified themselves as agnostic or atheist, the girls I interviewed were all from varieties of Christian backgrounds; this material should not be generalized to girls from other religious traditions. As part of the research design, however, I interviewed girls from as wide a variety of theological backgrounds, geographic locations, and economic circumstances as I could, to provide as comprehensive a view of the world of Christian girls' spirituality as I could.

During the four-year period between 1993 and 1997, I talked to over 100 girls from Boston, New York, Philadelphia, Dallas, Denver, Indianapolis, and Atlanta. Interviews took place in church youth groups, in dance troupes, in prep school lounges, and in a church "attic" with girls after an annual youth service. The girls represented diverse religious communities; they were Presbyterian, Methodist, Episcopalian, Roman Catholic, charismatic, Southern Baptist, agnostic, and those who categorized themselves as "nothing" or atheist. They also represented diverse ethnicities: Arab American, African American, Anglo, Eurasian, and Latina.

Chapter 1 describes the process of how we, as adults, can attempt to listen to girls. This process begins with remembering and, in some ways, reliving our own adolescent years. Most of us have buried pain and treasure from these years that need to be uncovered in order to understand our own feelings about the girls with whom we work. Listening to girls, most of whom are taught to hide true feelings and to disguise their own needs, requires special sensitivities and imposes ethical restraints.

In chapter 2 girls talk about their relationship to God and its importance in their lives. For most, God is a being who is close but could be closer. They describe ways in which they feel God supports them and ways in which God doesn't fulfill their expectations of someone with whom they are in relationship.

Girls develop their relationships to God in the context of their communities of faith. In chapter 3 girls describe the relationship of their own spiritualities to participation in their family churches. For most, belonging to a church also has both positive and negative aspects.

In chapter 4 girls talk about sexuality, their bodies, and the ways in which their spirituality influences their feelings about both. They also discuss the ways in which they relate to pressures from both their parents and boys on these issues.

Chapter 5 describes the girls' experience of and feelings about violence in their lives. Most girls have either experienced violence themselves or know close friends or family members who have been attacked or raped. Some have even experienced murders of those they love. Violence is an issue that girls seem reluctant to connect to spirituality; most don't know how to believe in a God who allows violent evil to take place.

* * *

The girls I interviewed exemplify other girls in many ways. They are articulate and sensitive. They think deeply about spiritual matters, and they consciously struggle to integrate their spiritualities with the rest of their lives. Hopefully, readers will find ideas and feelings expressed by these girls that will illuminate the lives of girls the readers know and love. Readers may find, as I have, that spirituality, far from being a marginal aspect of girls' lives, is the vibrant center of their chief hopes and fears, a clear measure of their strengths and vulnerabilities.

1 ✎

Listening to Ourselves, Listening to Girls

"Remember only this one thing," said Badger. "The stories people tell have a way of taking care of them. If stories come to you, care for them. And learn to give them away where they are needed. Sometimes a person needs a story more than food to stay alive. That is why we put those stories in each other's memory. This is how people care for themselves."

—from *Crow and Weasel,* Barry Lopez[1]

A girl's spirituality is never separate from the environment in which she grows. It develops out of relationships with important people and communities as well as with God. Girls' spiritualities are also always shaped and influenced by the cultures in which they develop. The ways in which a culture views girls, their families, their ethnicities, their intellectual abilities, their sexual orientations, their social expectations, and their religious traditions directly affect the ways in which girls' selves and spiritualities take shape.

LISTENING TO OURSELVES

Every year I teach a class for seminary students on counseling adolescents. Subjects covered in the class are fairly standard for a course of this type and range from developmental psychology, to biology, to sexuality, to spirituality. What is striking about students in the class, however, is the nervousness with which they approach the subject matter, because it is related to adolescents. Most, even those who are currently working with high school students in their churches, confess to having an uneasiness around or even fear of adolescents. Many, when they see the syllabus, and realize that they will be required to have extended conversations with a teenager as part of a longer assignment, express dread.

Many cultural factors account for this reaction to adolescents, I suspect—fears of violence from them, fears of coming into contact with aspects of the cultural underworld connected with uncontrolled hormones, bad judgment, and peer pressure (as if those forces don't have impact in adult culture!), fears of being misunderstood, fears of being laughed at, even perhaps fears of being forced to see their own more-or-less carefully constructed worlds in new ways. More than all this, however, I suspect that for many students fear of adolescents comes from anxieties about confronting aspects of their own teenage years that have been comfortably forgotten or forcibly buried, and that they, as adults, have no strong desire to remember or uncover. Being with teenagers often forces adults to relive aspects of their own pasts that they have spent enormous energy ejecting from everyday awareness. It is probably no accident that while many families hold their "baby books" of memories among their most cherished possessions, very few keep "teenage books" at all.

The first assignment I give students in this class is to write brief accounts of some important aspect of their own teenage years. Many write of traumas, although that is not specifically the assignment, and a good portion tell me that they cry all the way through the writing. As the class progresses, most begin to remember the good aspects of their lives at that time, aspects that have invariably been buried alongside or underneath the more negative ones. By the end of the class, most feel more comfortable with the teenagers they come into contact with in their work, and most indicate they feel they have integrated an important missing piece into their personal narratives and self-understanding.

A great many of the students also recover aspects of their understandings of religion and God from their adolescent years and are able to see their current theologies and spiritualities in light of this very formative time in their religious development. Often they are surprised to see that their religious experiences have many layers and are not entirely either good or evil. While positive aspects often were predominant, their spiritual histories from adolescence also held shadowy surprises for them: views of God that were oppressive, aspects of their church communities that were dangerous and negative, relationships with people who misunderstood them and sometimes took advantage of their enthusiasm and gratitude.

Part of the impetus for this study came from my reflections on my own late childhood and adolescent spirituality. I did not call it spirituality then. I thought of it as "my beliefs."

I can remember struggling with these beliefs—trying to make them fit my life meaningfully and trying to alter my life (mostly unsuccessfully) to fit them. When I look back, I see that what felt at the time like merely cognitive decisions involved much more. My experience of refining my beliefs involved my whole being— my relationships to family, friends, and church, my sexuality, my body, and my psyche, along with my thinking about and relationship to God. It involved remarkable personal affirmations and encouragement from others; it also involved devastating betrayals and even challenges to my emotional health.

The narratives of my spiritual journey through adolescence are—like most other people's—unremarkable in most ways, and exceptional in other ways. Like most people's lives, especially during adolescence, the different narratives don't fit together easily. Most people, especially at the early stages of reflection about their lives, tend to separate the positive from the negative aspects. Many prefer to tell one story or the other. But even in their efforts to separate the stories, elements of the negative infect the positive, and vice versa—it is impossible to separate them fully. To tell the story truly all of the elements of all of the strands need to be included.

To tell my story, and to highlight the differences, I have separated the strands as much as possible in the following three narratives. I include my own story because I believe that everyone who works with girls needs to "come clean" to others (if not to the girls) about their own spiritual experience as an adolescent. Hopefully, hearing my story will help the reader not only to understand the context of this volume, but also to see the multifaceted character of what we call spirituality.

Strand 1: Affirmation and Nurture

My home town, nestled in the northern suburbs of Chicago, was a beautiful place in the late 1960s and early 1970s. Kids walked to neighborhood schools down tree-covered streets and knew most everyone they encountered on the way. Christmases were snowy; summers were spent swimming and sunning at the local lake. Our dads were mostly successful, our mothers were mostly attentive and kind. Any alcoholism, domestic violence, or abuse was well hidden. Most of us felt that our community was in some ways charmed.

The First Presbyterian Church in my town was the context of much of my religious experience during this time. It was the third place my family visited when we moved to town in 1966—the summer before my sixth-grade year. After finding the library and the grocery store, my mother made sure we had a church. Within a month I was invited to play the piano for the fourth-through-sixth grade Sunday school. My first Sunday at the church I met a friend who was to become one of the only people I ever trusted with all my secrets.

Peg Davis (same name as my mother) and I met on an errand to find glue in the church kitchen. She was the only kid I'd ever met who got kicked out of Sunday school for asking too many

questions. I was always horrified and intrigued by her man-
ners—asking hard questions always seemed rude to me—and I
felt sorry for the teachers who were terribly overmatched in
their encounters with her.

In addition to a best friend, the church introduced me to
boys. It became the safe place to begin to enjoy the company
and touch of the "guys" at slowdances and hayrides. My eighth-
grade summer substitute teacher, the excruciatingly handsome
son of the high school physics teacher, smoked cigarettes in
class and taught us about Walden Pond.

The church also provided outlets for intellectual and physical
needs. The annual book sale provided Peg and me an afternoon
or two a year of pure delight sorting through old paperbacks (a
dime each) and hours of reading pleasure for otherwise un-
eventful summer days. The annual rummage sale provided fan-
ciful old clothes for high school and (after I was married, and my
husband was in seminary) baby clothes for my daughter.

The church was also an entrance to a world of beauty and
art. The 11:00 P.M. Christmas Eve service—standing for the
"Hallelujah Chorus" and passing the candles' flame during
"Silent Night"—provided a new kind of magic for Christmas
seasons left sadly empty by the demise of the beliefs in magic
elves and reindeer.

The First Presbyterian Church provided a center for family
and friends, a place for exploration and discovery, a safe place
for children and teenagers. It was a place where adults valued
children. It was a place I loved to be.

Strand 2: Unanswered Questions and Terror

I may have been more serious about religious things than my
friends, but I'm not sure. Although we mostly didn't talk
about it until some of our friends were drafted, my adolescence took place during the war in Vietnam. It was also the
time of the energized Civil Rights Movement and the women's
movement; the time of Jimi Hendrix, Cream, and Janis Joplin.

All of us, it seemed, had pretty good questions about God's relationship to world events when we got a chance to talk. Very few of these questions were ever heard, however; almost none were answered.

My first big religious question was occasioned by confirmation class at church. All of us in the class were seventh graders from the town's one public junior high school. Most of us were less enthused about the class than our parents were, but we were fairly well-behaved. Our teacher was the courtly old, pipe-smoking senior pastor whose Sunday-only Scottish brogue and trembling, energy-infused voice held our community in thrall week after week. None of us at the time realized that our parents were anxious in the presence of this man and his power. We just struggled to stay attentive.

This seemingly nonthreatening class, however, provoked my first religious crisis: how could I pledge my life to a God in whom I wasn't sure I believed? Especially in the form presented to me by this man? Shouldn't an oath like the one the church was asking me to make in confirmation be undertaken only after years of study? Shouldn't we at least be presented with other alternatives?

Fearing that my question would not be taken seriously by the teacher or the class, I quietly checked out a book on world religions, which I found in the church library. This book discouraged me; I didn't have the knowledge or tools to begin a comparative study of religion. I looked at the pictures, read the statistics about numbers of devotees in various locations, and made my first religious decision: to resign myself to becoming a member of the church of the only God readily available to me. I formally became a Presbyterian on Maundy Thursday 1968.

After the service, my father (a lawyer, who was less wholeheartedly Presbyterian than my mother but who was the only of my family to attend) asked me half-kiddingly, "So, you feel any different?" "Nope," I replied. That was the last said by anyone about my confirmation. Later, I realized that he probably wondered about the oath and the meaning of confirmation too.

In high school my Presbyterian beliefs were energized by reading Jonathan Edwards's "Sinners in the Hands of an Angry God," which I took very seriously and which therefore terrified me. These beliefs and fears were readily undone by the refreshingly positive philosophy of Ralph Waldo Emerson, introduced by a smart and cynical sophomore English teacher. Emerson's idea of the Oversoul (which didn't seem to care about doctrine, and certainly didn't throw souls into hell) was a huge relief.

In the fall of my junior year in high school a new youth pastor introduced two ideas troubling to my spirituality: the idea of being "saved" and the reality of demons. It took me a while to believe in the necessity of salvation, but the talk of demons terrorized me (as much as Edwards's sermon had) with thoughts of damnation, evil, and hell. I began to hate driving alone at night for fear of demons showing themselves in the rearview mirror. I developed a deep phobia about sleeping alone and tormented my younger sister by crawling into her very small bed with her when my night terrors became overwhelming.

It was not until my sophomore year in college that I was able to resolve both of the spiritual issues introduced by my youth pastor: when I got "saved" into the Lighthouse, a fellowship of Jesus freaks dedicated to the eradication of Satan and his works on earth. My moment of salvation came as the community was singing a mournful song about the "rapture": "There's no time to change your mind, the Son has come and you've been left behind."

The Jesus freaks, with their strange theologies, welcomed me and gave me a chance to explore some of the more sensual aspects of Christianity: candles burning in a dark warehouse meeting room, (re)baptism in a cold and muddy lake, speaking in tongues, worshiping with raised hands, and great feasts with local churches. It was an insular community where we knew each other deeply—smelly shoes, haircuts, intestinal flu, and phone bills were all matters of concern and prayer. Caring for homeless and crazy people, witnessing on the streets, and Bible studies created great diversions of energy from other more normal college-age pursuits (including studying).

Nevertheless, on the night of my "salvation," just before raising my hand—my second public religious oath in four years—I remember thinking, "If I become serious about this, I will lose my mind . . ."

Three years later, I was 22 with a husband and a new baby, when the fruits of our neo-pentecostal theology finally erupted into my psychological life with devastating effect. I had graduated from college and wanted to begin to work to help support our family. But the conservative church we had joined when the Lighthouse disbanded forbade it. God ordained wives and mothers to stay at home with their children. It was, in fact, a shame on the family and the church if a woman worked outside of the home. I secretly began longing to leave—home, church, and God—and I began to have dizzy spells and panic attacks, becoming deathly afraid of shopping, driving, speaking out loud in public, and especially of attending church. I feared that I might faint, or worse, begin screaming during worship. I felt that death or insanity was closing in on me. At its worst, I stopped driving, attending church, going on walks with my daughter, having guests, or visiting others. I stopped venturing outside the door of our little roach-filled student apartment. I shut the door and hid.

Years later an article my mother sent me named my condition and those fears agoraphobia. At the time, I had no name for the craziness and despair I was feeling. I went to bed at night waiting for God to kill me because of my longings to leave. During the day, I fantasized about dying. I lived this way for almost eighteen months, until the lure of attending classes in the religious studies department at Indiana University became stronger than my fears. Studying was something even my judgmental god would not deny me.

Strand 3: Abuse in the Community

The third strand of my narrative is just as troubling. It illuminates another side of the First Presbyterian Church—not one I experienced directly, but one that provided undercurrents of the entire community's life together.

The church was the place where a close friend of mine was repeatedly sexually molested in the basement by his Sunday school teacher as a "punishment for bad behavior" in the classroom. He was told not to tell his parents or anyone else, because it was "his fault." My friend lived with the terror of those memories into adulthood before he could reveal what had been done to him. Even now, he refuses to attend church or to send his children. The church was also the place where a staff member was having abusive sexual relationships with parishioners who trusted him to be their spiritual counselor. He was eventually quietly dismissed. He quickly began working at another church in another state.

* * *

My adolescent spirituality was the same as and different from other people's. I was entranced by and energized by my childhood church, even as my questions were left unspoken and unanswered. I was particularly vulnerable to some kinds of spiritual distortions; I took certain parts of reformed theology more seriously than others did, and I was unconvinced by declarations of God's grace. Neo-pentecostal and evangelical theology was, for me, in large part a prison, but I appreciated the seriousness with which my "brothers and sisters in Christ" took their beliefs and the cultural critiques they formulated.

My adolescent spirituality was, as anyone's, multi-layered, containing multiple meanings. Many different kinds of narratives could be developed to describe it—both negative and positive. It can be understood as a psychological journey, as well as a spiritual one. If I had told the story with all the strands joined, if the story could be seen as single narrative, it would be clear that my struggles to be in relationship with God and a faith community both sustained me and endangered me. My adolescent spirituality provided both the storm and the ballast for my life.

LISTENING TO GIRLS

One of the major concerns of adolescent girls—documented in academic studies,[2] in fiction written *for* girls,[3] in writing by girls,[4] and in best-selling books about girls[5]—is that girls have trouble being understood and being taken seriously by the adult world that has so much power over them. Girls, in fact, often feel that telling what they believe or think, expressing preferences, lobbying for what they want, or asking for what they need are dangerous enterprises. This is related to what educators call a hidden curriculum[6] in the culture that teaches girls in subtle ways that they are not important.

Included in this hidden curriculum is the rule that girls must be *nice*, even when they are feeling nasty or are angry, and even when they are threatened. The niceness rule invalidates girls' feelings, and often leads girls to question their own experience and even sanity. Mary Pipher puts it succinctly: "Girls who speak frankly are labeled as bitches." And, as one of the girls she interviews says, "That will shut anyone up."[7]

Many girls I interviewed expressed deep discomfort with themselves and the level of coherence between their inner selves and their public demeanor. Katy, an eighteen-year-old from New York, said it well:

> *If I could change one thing about myself now it would be being more honest. I am honest but sometimes I say things I'm not sure I really believe. I know I need to be more honest with God . . . and not to say things I don't really believe.*

Her tendency not to tell what she really believed was her most profound dissatisfaction with herself.

Latoya Hunter, a twelve-year-old African American girl, who kept a diary (later published) of her first year in junior high school writes of her determination to say the truth and be heard by her parents:

October 11, 1990

I talked to Isabelle today. Remember she had that problem with her mother? Well, she finally worked up the nerve to talk to her mother and what do you know? She's grounded. Just because she gave her opinion. Isabelle's really frustrated now. I could understand why. I've told you that most of my opinions don't check with my parents. If I had a problem I don't even think I'd talk to them about it. They'd just say, "When I was your age I could never talk to my mother and tell her anything like that."

What can I say? Parents just don't understand. It's no use to try to make them. It'll just backfire on you. Most kids would give up on trying to get understanding on both their parent's side, but not me. I'm a very stubborn girl. I explain my case from all sides. I try every trick in the book just to get approval on an issue.[8]

For Latoya, being heard is an exhausting task. From her perspective it involves disruption of her relationship with parents, enduring condescension, and facing possible punishment. As she notes, she is a "stubborn" girl who refused to give up—even to the point of having her work published! Many others, however, are not so persistent, or find the dangers not worth the risks. Many of them forget that they have anything important to say. A common response to my requests to do interviews with girls is: "Why would you want to know what *I* believe?"

Carol Gilligan, a distinguished scholar and advocate for girls, writes about her experience interviewing adolescent girls. When the girls would be willing to take her into their confidences, she often felt that she was entering an "underground world" where girls led her to "caverns of knowledge, which then suddenly were covered over, as if nothing was known and nothing was happening."[9] Girls were nervous talking with her, even though her work involved the promotion of their values.

For those girls, no one deserved instant or complete access, no matter what their credentials or intentions.

In light of this, my goal in interviewing girls about their spiritualities was twofold. First, I wanted to learn something about the caverns in girls' underground spiritual worlds and to share that knowledge with other adults. The hope is that with this understanding parents, teachers, and youth leaders can be more responsive to girls and their spiritual journeys. The second goal was to give girls a platform from which they might be honest, be safe, and be taken seriously.

Talking frankly about spiritual experiences creates special kinds of vulnerabilities. When a girl lets outsiders into her very private spiritual life, it means she is granting a privilege that might not be respected. She might be ridiculed, disbelieved, or even punished. The knowledge might be shared with those who could hurt her or use it against her. Talking with girls has, ironically, led me to a profound respect for their silences and wariness and for the parts of the stories that are not told. Protected areas are necessary. The stories shared with me are rich but also full of contradictions and gaps. Some of them don't make sense as they stand; some obviously need an interpretive key; some may only be partially true; some reflect Katy's struggle to be honest even when it doesn't feel natural.

For a girl to tell the truth about her spirituality is an act of courage and resistance. She must believe in her own story; she must be willing to take her story seriously even when others wouldn't; she must be willing to talk about things that most girls are not generally accustomed to discussing. To speak honestly, which most of the girls seemed to want to do, they must be willing to negate a deeply embedded cultural rule about merely being nice.

I saw my responsibility as a researcher to be fourfold: *First* to avoid coercion in the interview process. As researchers know, it *is* possible to force people to tell stories that they don't want to tell, by intimidation, by subtle promises and threats, and by other forms of manipulation such as flattery. Coercion is the opposite of empowerment, however. Coercion had to be avoided as much as possible, because if these interviews were forced they would subvert the goal of helping girls to talk safely and to be heard. Girls need to have the right to remain silent.

Because I came into the girls' lives from the outside,[10] from a position of relative power (being an adult and a professor of theology), and sponsored by important people in their lives (parents and church leaders), I recognized that many might feel that they *had* to participate in my research if asked. Most girls seemed genuinely eager and willing to participate. Other girls found ways to avoid participating without having directly to say no. Some agreed to participate and then didn't show up at the appointed time. These girls were not called or followed up on, unless they called me to reschedule. Some forgot or didn't have time to complete questionnaires; this was respected. Some gave vague, bored, or very incomplete answers. Although I didn't detect it, some may have fabricated most of their answers.

In addition to respecting girls' indirect messages that they didn't wish to participate, it was necessary to allow girls to be interviewed at the depth where they felt most comfortable—not pushing for information or stories beneath that level. Some girls stayed at a very surface level; most seemed to feel comfortable at an intermediate place—a place I fathomed was just below niceness; several felt secure enough to speak at a profound depth—out of hidden places, where insecurities and ambivalence and anger and confusion were manifest along with joy and awe and serenity. For the last group, niceness was not as important a constraint.

Sometimes protecting girls from coercion meant not interviewing them. In one case, for example, I had a detailed discussion of the project with a father who was obviously concerned about his two daughters and their spiritual well-being. He was eager to have me interview the girls so that I could give him a report. I could foresee that even if he accepted the ground rules about my not revealing girls' stories without their permission, he probably would be tempted to pressure the girls into talking about what they had said. So, even though the girls were lively and enthusiastic and articulate, and seemed willing, I declined to interview them.

My *second responsibility* as a researcher was to respect the insights and stories being shared. This meant, for a time, to drop my role as teacher and "expert" and be receptive to the girls' visions of truth—even those that were wildly divergent from my own—even those that I saw as oppressive or potentially dangerous. In many cases, when the girls were patient enough to explain them to me, I was able to hear how their visions often supported more positive values than I would have, at first, imagined.

Lauren, a seventeen-year-old from Alaska, helped me to understand, for instance, that her pentecostal church's and her family's beliefs about the roles of men and women in the "Christian home" functioned to protect her and encourage her, even as, more negatively, it taught her that she was not to be a spiritual leader. While she sincerely believed that she should not aspire to preach or teach in the church, she was encouraged to take her education seriously, develop her gifts as a musician, and participate meaningfully in her family's life.

Lauren's parents gave her a sense of participation in the family business that is not common for most girls. The summer before her interview she had spent with her brothers and sisters on their father's fishing boat, working many long cold hours off the Alaskan coast to supplement the family income. This experience taught her that "I have muscles and stamina. I can keep going even when I want to give up and I'm really really tired."

I saw her faith community's doctrine of women's roles being subordinate to men's as harmful to women and girls. Her family spirituality, however (which included the negative aspects of the subordinate role for women), also functioned to empower her. It gave her the space to develop her talents; it gave her important and meaningful challenges that reinforced her sense of her own strength.

Another aspect of respecting stories is being open to the many ways they could be told. One Saturday morning as I was interviewing a group of six African American girls in their church, I could tell that they were discouraged with me. I wasn't asking the right questions, and I wasn't responding to the right things. Later I understood that they were trying to tell me how important their church choir and dance troupe were to them. I was trying to find out about other aspects of their lives. Finally, they invited me to attend the afternoon's rehearsals.

It was only when observing the girls' interactions with their leaders, and with the boys in the choir, that I could appreciate the joy and energy of their spirituality. Watching them dance together and encourage one another and appreciate one another's gifts was dazzlingly exciting. Seeing them "get into their sway" and hearing their intensity in singing with their choir director and the accompanying guitars and piano was the most important way I could know about their spiritualities.

I came to understand that interviews and questionnaires had limitations, and that if I wanted to find out about spirituality, I had to respect and be sensitive to the differing ways that girls wanted to reveal it.

The *third responsibility* I had (and have) as a researcher is to protect the confidentiality of the girls who took part. Each girl was told that her story would be told in a way that would not identify her. This involved changing names, locations, and identifying facts. It also involved not telling some stories that would identify girls no matter how much the minor facts were changed.

The *fourth responsibility* I have is to share their insights and stories as truthfully as I can, being responsible to their visions of themselves and the world. A major part of this responsibility was to become as fully aware of my own values as possible and of the ways in which these might impede my abilities to hear and tell the girls' stories. My beliefs about what is normal, healthy, dangerous, or oppressive shape the ways in which I hear and report stories. My liberal feminist Protestantism makes it more difficult for me to hear conservative and Roman Catholic girls fairly. The fact that I am white and middle class makes it more difficult for me to hear those of other ethnicities and economic/social levels. These characteristics also make it more difficult for me to hear girls who I perceive to be like me because I could easily hear their stories as being more similar to mine than they are.

I was with each girl no more than two hours, interviewing her and going over her questionnaires. Nevertheless, even in those brief encounters, the depth of their experience was clear. Their stories and insights clearly reflected struggles and joys in their spiritualities. They talked about faith, God, their churches, their families, their questions, and their doubts. They are angry and satisfied. They are wary and eager to trust. They are able to interpret their own experiences, but are grateful for those who can help. All of their stories are different, yet many have threads and themes in common. They are fascinating and intense. They deserve to be taken seriously and to be listened to respectfully.

2 ✒

Girls Talk about God

I don't feel separated from God, but instead he is my best friend. I talk to him about everything. At times I fear God, but I think that is good, so I won't forget his strength.

—Karyn, 17

God is very abstract to me—probably because no one ever sat me down and told me exactly what I should believe.

—Gena, 18

The biggest problem I have with God is that he doesn't answer back in your prayers.

—Annie, 11

A girl's spirituality radiates from her relationship with God. This relationship can be powerfully and positively influential in her life. If her spirituality is healthy, God is one to whom she turns for guidance, for comfort, for protection, and for connection. For many girls God is the one who is there "for me," who can be depended on to take their sides and to be there through crisis and change.

Being in positive relationship with God, however, is not the complete reality for many girls; there are ways in which God is seen as not being totally reliable or helpful. Indeed, for some girls, God seems almost cruel for what God allows to happen in the world and in their lives. In addition, girls talk about social problems associated with admitting to being a Christian, especially a conservative Christian, including being ostracized and misunderstood by other people.

Some girls have relationships with God that include mysterious elements—these girls report having seen visions, having strange feelings and intuitions, and having been comforted by gracious intermediaries between themselves and God. Some girls also talk about experiencing mysterious and powerful evil. This chapter brings to light the positive and negative effects that girls report of their relationship with God, as well as some of the special moments of grace and mystery.

GIRLS' SPIRITUAL WORLDS

Girls live in a different spiritual world than most adult church members; many girls live in dangerous environments, and they know it. If they have not been the victims of violence, they know friends and classmates who have been. Research on criminal victimization rates of girls has shown that one in three girls will be sexually abused before she is eighteen.[1] Of these girls, 89 percent have been abused by a family member.[2] The Department of Justice *National Crime Victimization Survey* from 1993 reports that girls ages 12–24 are almost ten times more likely to be raped than females of other ages.[3] Murder rates are also much higher for adolescents (both boys and girls) than for other age groups.[4] Undoubtedly some of girls' appreciation for horror stems from their relatively dangerous social locations in the culture.

Carol Gilligan writes that because girls are often victimized, impeded from having powerful voices, and disregarded as to their visions and understandings, they retreat to a metaphorically underground world.[5] She talks about meeting girls in their underground caverns of knowledge where they keep their most precious thoughts and insights. Girls stop living their lives on the surface of things. They stop talking out loud, but they don't stop thinking about relationships. They become experts in this field and theorize endlessly about things such as what is necessary to sustain relationships, what counts for betrayal, what levels of meaning are attached to actions, or what sorts of actions lead to what sorts of reactions. Girls become clear that relationships take place as much in the underground parts of life as in the clear air. Some of what takes place leads to happiness, and some contributes to a sense of horror.

Adults who tap into girls' fascination with the underground sides of life make a very good living. The best selling young-adult author of all time, R. L. Stine, churns out little novels authenticating this vision almost every other day.[6] V. C. Andrews writes more substantial novels about girls whose lives are touched by evil and marked by their resistance to it.[7]

Books about girls who are addicted to drugs,[8] are in love with serial killers,[9] are sexually abused,[10] and are living with physically abusive relatives[11] are currently among girls' favorites. Both the *New York Times*[12] and *Publishers Weekly*[13] have run articles recently wondering about girls' predilections for such grim topics.

From their underground caverns, girls see and live in a part of life that most adults, especially those of us who consider ourselves churchpeople, don't regularly allow ourselves to see—except when we allow Stephen King or Anne Rice onto our bedside tables. It is only natural that girls would gravitate to books and literature that validate their own vision.

Mark Edmundson, an English literature professor at the University of Virginia, published an excellent volume of provocative popular theology entitled *Nightmare on Main Street*. In his book he attempts to explain the resurgence of what he calls gothic horror in North American culture generally.[14] He writes that he found himself strangely drawn to a whole set of current and cult horror movies—with titles like *Scream, Dawn of the Dead, Last House on the Left, Nightmare on*

Elm Street, and *Texas Chainsaw Massacre.* He not only watched these films, he became somewhat obsessed with them. Then he tried to figure out why.

In brief, Edmundson decided that he had tapped into a cultural undercurrent (almost undertow) of horror—gothic horror—"possession narratives" running from the O. J. Simpson trial to *The Oprah Winfrey Show,* to horror movies, to rumors of ritual cult abuse, to the *X-Files,* to the evening news.

Gothic, Edmundson writes, "is the art of haunting. . . . It shows us time and again that life, even at its most ostensibly innocent is possessed, that the present is in thrall to the past. All are guilty. All must, in time, pay up."[15]

Why this undercurrent of horror? Edmundson's almost throwaway answer is that people have stopped believing in God:

> Though most of us Americans claim to believe in God, few of us seem able to believe in God's presence. That is, we do not perceive some powerful force for good shaping the events of day-to-day life in accord with a perceptibly benevolent master plan. Most of us don't have a story that we can believe about the way God's designs are unfolding among us. Whatever God is up to, he is not busying himself unduly with worldly events.[16]

How can we escape the horror of a godless world? Edmundson notes another strong undercurrent in our culture—one he identifies with angels and *Forrest Gump*—which he calls "facile transcendence." Forrest, the main character, is faced with many challenges and heartbreaking circumstances, but none touch his essential goodness. And he is richly rewarded for remaining simple. Edmundson writes, "Through [all his trials] Alabaman Forrest is magnolia sweet. . . . At the core of Forrest Gump is the sugary fiction that dull virtue in tandem with humble, unresenting poverty is well rewarded."[17]

Forrest Gump is an archetype for the culture's need for a vacation from horror. He is the respite—to whom we turn when we need a breath of cleaner air. The air is not satisfying because it's too sweet. But it's some sort of relief.

* * *

In a move more complex than Edmundson might give them credit for, many girls' spiritualities combine both a sense of a loving and caring God with the sense that God is dangerous or unreliable. Their God is rarely of the Forrest Gump kind—for most of these girls God is good but not sweet. Many of the girls in this study also bear witness to a gothic vision of the world arising from their own experience, their view from the underground, and their cultural heritage. They are struggling, perhaps more honestly than most adults, to find a way to believe in a real God in the real world.

A POSITIVE RELATIONSHIP WITH GOD

Being in a relationship, for girls, involves honest and open communication—people in relationships listen to each other, respond to each other's needs, and speak truthfully about all important issues. For many of the girls, God is a person with whom they are in relationship, but it is not a simple one. Though each girl's relationship is different, common features arise in interviews. When girls talked about positive aspects of their relationship with God, they often mentioned such things as being taken care of in crisis situations, being taught how to live, being encouraged to do good things for others, and being healed when tragedy entered their lives.

Unconditional Love

At this point in their lives, when they are experimenting with identity and with relationality, it is important that girls find those who accept them, day to day, for who they are becoming. God seems to be a person, for many of them, who they can call a friend—a person who can ride out the bumps with them, who will understand the good they do and the problems they get themselves into. God takes them as they are. Mary expresses this when she talks about God's unconditional love:

> Mary: *One of the most important beliefs in my life is that God loves me unconditionally. It's just extremely comforting.*

Q: What does "unconditionally" mean for you?

> Mary: *Without criticism. I mean, God won't say, "You're a bad person because . . ." Even when you screw up there's somebody to love you.*

Other girls talked about how grateful they were that God was there for them when they were going through self-admittedly rough times:

> Cheryl (17): *I felt closest to God this past year and a half. I was messed up, and then I accepted God. My dad went to jail, and my best friend died, etc. So I was having a very hard time.*

God helped her to live through her own time of struggling and through other serious and sad experiences. She talked about her humiliation that her father was in jail and the great grief of losing a friend. When she "accepted" God, God was there for her through the hard times.

Karyn (17) feels that she can be close to God, through Jesus, because Jesus was a person who experienced pain like she does:

> *Jesus Christ is very important to me, because he is the link between me and God. I don't feel intimidated talking to Christ since he experienced being a man on Earth, and underwent tremendous pain. I know he understands my everyday problems.*

Jesus is a person who can be trusted; her everyday problems will not be too much for him, because he has proven himself by going through tremendous pain as a human. She isn't intimidated by him because he knows, and thus, understands, something of her life.

Unconditional love involves not only the resolve to keep loving someone no matter what they do, it also involves the strength and understanding to keep one's resolution. These girls experience God as someone who has promised to be there for them through the hardest of "messed up" times, through their own mistakes, and in spite of their "screw ups." In addition, as Karyn states, these are not empty promises; Jesus has undergone the experience of being a person and knows what pain and suffering feel like. He has been tested.

God Teaches Girls about Their Lives

Often girls spoke about God or Jesus giving them a model for the way they should live their own lives. Linda calls herself "handi-capable" due to a genetic disorder that affects her ability to walk and gives her a short stature. She became closer to God after going to college, where she became a participant and leader in campus worship. As part of her daily worship, she began to experiment with different forms of prayer and meditation:

> Linda (19): *I got closer to God while I was doing the spiritual exercises of St. Ignatius. It was a semester-long commitment, and it's a lot of reflection. And, basically, it teaches you a new way to pray. Instead of formal prayer, a lot of it is reading Bible passages and reflecting on those. And a lot of it too is conversations with God, describing your emotions at that time.*

Out of this, and in response to theology classes she was taking, she developed a new respect for the person of Jesus. She was especially excited about Jesus' treatment of the poor and those who were socially or physically different:

> *Jesus . . . his life is a model for me. He had respect for everyone, and showed how to give yourself in service, and how to take care of the poor. I think God expects me to imitate Jesus in that.*

Q: Talk a little about respect and what that means.

I think with my own self, with being physically challenged, that the stares that you get from people—comments that people make really bother me. With little kids it's excusable, because they're curious. But things that adults do aren't excusable. And I think that a lot of people are very afraid of someone who's different, whether it be color, or physical size, or walking capability, physical mobility, whatever . . . that just really ticks me off.

Q: People are rude?

Yeah, they can be.

Q: So, for you it's important to be tolerant of all sorts of differences?

Yeah, nobody is the same. Actually, an activity I know is to have people sit down and say, "Everyone in this room is special. What's special about you?"

My mother never called me "defective." I've always been "handicapable." My parents have always treated me normal—that I can do anything anyone else can do. I know my limitations. I know when to say, "I need help with this, or I can't do this."

But, as far as most things go, I can do pretty much everything.

Linda's relationship to her parents and her attachment to Jesus as a model have helped her to see herself in a positive light, despite social pressure and rudeness from children and adults. She talks about wanting to devote her life to working for the poor; at the time of the interview she was involved in working with the Catholic Worker Movement clinic in her city and with a daycare program for children from the inner city. Jesus' life has become a model for her own.

* * *

Another sort of lesson girls learned from God was that crisis times in their lives might be God's disciplining or testing of them. These times were meant to help them gain a new and more realistic perspective on life. The following girls, from a rural community that has undergone severe economic distress in the past several years, try to make sense of the hardship by discussing God's purposes:

> Amanda (13): *People lose money, and they lose their houses, and they lose their families and stuff like that. And they don't have much money to do anything, you know, and only one car between them. And they've had a lot of troubles in their lives, and it takes them awhile to bounce back. But I think God is testing them to see their beliefs . . . if they'll keep faith.*
>
> *I think that's why he does it—to see if they'll keep their faith in him after taking everything they've had—their pride and joy—and if they'll still believe in him. I think that's what he does.*

A shadowy side of God begins to appear. This is a God who will take away people's pride and joy in order to see if they will remain faithful. This is the God of Job who requires loyalty even in the face of trouble and testing.

Q: Isn't that kind of mean?

> Amanda: *In a way, but in a way, no. I think he wants them to learn. A lot of people think they made their money all on their own, but a lot of time God . . . it's his, and he's given it to them. So a lot of people are like, "Oh, I built my house by myself," you know, and "It's my money, and I earned all my money by myself." I mean, God helped you do the things you did, and if it wasn't for him, a lot of people wouldn't have the stuff they do have. But I think he tests you a lot.*

In taking things from people, God is not being mean; God is trying to teach them that they are not self-sufficient. If people forget to whom they owe their belongings and their financial success, God will test them to make sure they remember that God was the one who provided.

Mary (14): *I don't think God is mean. It's like when your parents punish you; they're doing it out of love. And I think God's doing it out of love to show you that you're not perfect, and you can't make it by yourself. It's almost a way of him showing that "If you're going to keep on trying to be all-powerful and if you think you're on top of the world—you're not!" You can't try to be God.*

God punishes as a loving parent would, in order to show people their limitations. People might forget who they are— begin to think that they are as powerful as God, or without need of God's help—if God didn't remind them that they're not all powerful or perfect.

Amanda: *I agree with her. I don't think God's mean. He does put you through a lot, but I think He's just trying to test your faith in him, and when you do have strong faith in God, things go better for you. He just wants everyone to have strong faith.*

Again, Amanda rejects the notion that God is mean. God's testing is all for your own good, so "things [will] go better for you." Her community's struggles have a meaning. Strong faith means good self-understanding, including understanding one's limitations. Strong faith gives one humility in the face of God's providence. Strong faith sometimes requires hard testing.

Moving Closer to God

Several girls talked about their desire to establish a closer relationship to God. They talked about feeling a lack in their lives when they could not go to God easily, whether through prayer or sacraments. One girl expressed a tentative hope that she would be able to incorporate spirituality into her life even though she cannot remember a time when she believed in God.

* * *

Meredith is 15. She goes to a very conservative private school where religion is central to the school's life and ethos. She and her family, however, do not attend church, and she does not consider herself a religious person. Nevertheless, her image of God is both beautiful and tender:

God is like a tree to me, because it represents life. It is a source of life to many creatures, a provider or nurturing character. A tree is large and provides shelter. The roots stretch far under the surface of the ground.

She is both proud and a bit timid about her newfound desire to attend worship. Her family has not encouraged her or forced her in either direction. She is proud to make her own decision but afraid to move forward without them, "by myself":

Although I don't go to church, sometimes I feel that I need to or want to. No one in my family makes me go, so it would be my own decision to go by myself.

Part of her desire is an experience she had with a church group on retreat, where she began to think about what it might mean to dedicate herself to Jesus:

I went on a church retreat a few months ago where they asked you to dedicate yourself to Jesus. I did not stand up like some people did, but it really started me thinking about my faith in God. Now, I feel that I am slowly moving closer to God, which is what I would like to do.

She was not part of the group of people who rose on that occasion, because she didn't feel ready. Her approach to God is more measured and thoughtful. *I am slowly moving closer . . .* This, she makes clear, is her choice also; she will not allow herself to be pushed by her peers or discouraged by her family.

Slowly she moves toward what she believes will give her life, and nurture, shelter, and protection.

* * *

Elizabeth (18) from the same school was experiencing doubts. Her faith had grown less meaningful to her, and she was questioning God's existence. She was able to rediscover the meaning of her faith in the work she did at an inner-city youth camp:

I was doubting my faith this past summer. Through a contact I made doing service work, I got a volunteer opportunity for the summer to be a counselor at a Christian day camp in the inner city, called the Youth Project. The people I worked with were phenomenal Christians. They got me to start praying more often and they gave thanks to God in all circumstances. I really loved the kids, and I hope that we instilled in them the importance of God in their lives. I'm thinking about continuing a weekend youth group down there for the kids with some other counselors. I really was taught a lot by them and tested a lot by them, and it strengthened my faith.

Working with people who prayed and gave thanks to God in tough situations helped her to find meaning in her own faith. Serving children and helping them to find the importance of God helped her to rediscover how important God was in her own life. In order to continue to stay connected with God, she intended to continue her work of service.

Other girls also talked about the importance of service for their faith. Linda, above, saw service of the poor to be her calling in life, after the model of Jesus. Jeny (16), from a wealthy church in Atlanta, talked about seeing God in poor children:

The summer before last, I had the opportunity to travel with my youth group to do mission work in Jamaica. Through my experiences with the children, we were exposed to the presence of God.

Liz (15), from a large midwestern church, also spoke of a time at workcamp as being the period in her life when she felt closest to God:

When I was at senior high workcamp and convention this last summer with my youth group, I really felt God's presence. We worshiped together, and we did our best to help other people. We shared our experiences we'd had concerning God and talked of God's will for us.

Many girls in the study reported that their strongest feelings of being close to God came as they participated in work and service events. They learned lessons about their own situations in life, and the necessity to follow Christ's example. They reported seeing God in the faces of poor children, and of learning lessons from these children about toughness, as well as survival, humor, and strength.

* * *

Kate is a soft-spoken eighteen-year-old from New York City. Although her parents are wealthy and prominent figures in the city, Kate has been taught not to put herself forward. Her parents are not religious, so Kate was not taken to church as a child. She has also taken a path of service to bring her closer to God; her service is participating and leading worship at her school. She had been worried about the fact that she was never baptized and wondered whether or not she should receive communion. Previous to the year of the interview, she had been afraid:

> I felt closest to God when I first took communion. I'm not baptized, so I never felt like I could take communion. But one Sunday when I was taking part in the chapel service, and I was giving communion to others, I felt like it was my chance to take communion, and now I always take it.

Her approach to God has been cautious. She doesn't want to break any of the rules about what she should and should not be able to do. Finally, however, as she served communion to others, she got the courage to take it herself. She took her chance and put herself right with God, even though she was not officially sanctioned to receive the sacrament. This was the moment in her life when she felt closest to God. Now she takes communion regularly.

* * *

Mary Ellen is eighteen and is also from New York. She talks about never having believed in God, even when she was a small child. She speaks strongly, in clipped phrases, and has a very hard time speaking about painful experiences, such as her parents' divorce or their subsequent confiding in her about their marital problems. Any pain is covered over with "I'm fine!"

I never believed in God. I don't remember ever believing in God. My parents made me go every Sunday to Sunday school. . . . Both of my parents are really strong religious people. When I go home I don't go to church now, because they're divorced. It's not like we go to church as a family anymore—it happened the winter of my ninth-grade year. When I came home on the long weekend is when they told me. I was fine. I was upset at first, but I knew it was coming . . . it was just the realization that it was actually happening. That was upsetting. But after that I was fine, and ever since then I've been fine.

I get along better with both of them after the divorce. My father and I are more on the same level. He comes to me with problems too. Both my parents come to me for advice, if they're having a little problem with each other. I'm used to it now. I don't let it get to me. I hear it and I shrug it off. They both say the same stuff, like: "He was the one who wanted a divorce." "She was the one who wanted the divorce." I just sort of sit there, and I say, "Oh, come on."

She is willing to admit, a little sarcastically, that when she is afraid she clings to an idea that might protect her. She is deathly afraid of airplanes and often thinks of God when she has to fly:

I feel closest to God when I'm in a plane. I'll believe anything when I'm really afraid. (Laughs.) *Then I hope there is a God.*

Then, more seriously and wistfully:

I just don't believe that God is up there watching down on me.

Her real fear is fear of death; it is a fear that she has been dealing with since she was very young:

I wish I wasn't so afraid of death. It used to be really bad; it used to be huge. But I don't think about it that much any more. Between fifth and eighth grade I would have to sleep with my parents sometimes. It just really upset me. Since I don't know when it's going to happen. . . . I can't imagine, like, not being there. I've been thinking about that forever.

Lately, she is less afraid, because she has discovered a way to think of death that is less terrifying for her:

Now I think of it like when I'm going to sleep. You don't know exactly when you're going to sleep, so I won't know when I die. Because if I don't believe that I'm going to be up there, seeing people, then I'll never know anyway.

She hopes that she will see her grandparents after death. She believes that they are constantly watching her from above, and that thought comforts her. She will be going to college at Princeton in the fall and expects that her life will change in many ways. She says it feels good that her grandparents will see her go.

Q: Do you ever envision a time in your life when spirituality will be important?

Not really. But the cathedral at Princeton is really really beautiful, so I could see myself picking up religion when I go there. When I'm out of here. I'm looking forward to it. I feel like maybe I should just try it when I get there. I could see myself spending time in there. I don't have time here to think about it.

Mary Ellen is double-minded about death, her parents, and her spirituality. She has had great fears of death, and of becoming "nothing but a rotting body." She believes that she will just "not be here" after death; but she also hopes that she will see her grandparents, and she believes that they are looking out for her. She talks about her parents being very religious people, but their religion never made sense to her, even from her earliest childhood. At the end, she expresses a kind of longing for a more spiritual life, connected with the beauty of the chapel at Princeton. "I could see myself spending time in there." One hopes (against hope) that she will find the time to explore this path, in the midst of her busy life at college.

* * *

Girls begin to move closer to real relationships with God through personal courage to resist pressures to conform to more common forms of spirituality. Meredith moves slowly and deliberately toward a God who she believes will provide nurture and shelter to her; Elizabeth and others renew their faith, and discover deeper ways of connecting with God through service to the poor; Kate takes a step of personal courage and allows herself to come closer to God in a sacrament she believes the church would forbid; and Mary Ellen has vague dreams of becoming a more spiritual person. These girls inch toward relationship with God as they come to understand more about themselves, their needs, and their purposes in life.

God Provides Solace in Time of Crisis

One of the most important features of girls' relationship with God is their discernment that God carries them through times of crisis in their lives. Developmental theorist Robert Kegan describes the psychological impact of growth and change as moving from one kind of security ("culture of embeddedness") to another. As a girl grows and changes in adolescence, she naturally moves from one way of being to another. While she is changing, she is in a state of insecurity, in which important, stable figures can give her a sense of safety and permanence. Kegan writes of an interaction he had with his own daughter while she was in the midst of a shift:

> She came to look for a parent, and sought to initiate what I suggest is the hardest kind of conversation, because rather than the first requirement of human interaction—the presentation of a coherent

self—her conversation is about the very inability to be any longer coherent; she is presenting instead two selves, not because she is crazy, but because she is evolving.[18]

While Kegan's daughter came to him for help in finding a secure place to "rest," many adolescent girls seem to turn to God. They are especially likely to turn to God in times of crisis, and they are grateful for the stability God provides.

* * *

Riki (18) from Houston says that she felt closest to God at the time of an automobile accident, after she had just had her license for two days:

I felt closest to God when I wrecked my car. I really wanted to die and go to heaven. It sounds a little corny, but it's the worst trouble I've ever been in, and I needed serious help. I think I'm defining "closest" as a point when I've actually talked to God (in my head) for lengthy periods of time.

I wanted to die. It was really bad, even though I didn't hurt myself, I was in really bad trouble. I ran a stop sign—no one got hurt. Now I look back on it and I know that I shouldn't have wished that God would get me out of trouble. It all worked out—maybe it was God, and maybe it was something else. I shouldn't have wished it, because people are in worse trouble than that.

She now looks back and wonders whether it was really God who got her out of trouble. But at the time she spent hours in prayer, wondering how she would ever repay her parents or regain their trust. She also wonders whether she should have "wasted God's time" with a need like hers when she observes others with much bigger problems. She cannot even remember the power of the need she felt for assistance at her time of insecurity.

* * *

Allyson (15) felt closest to God when her father, a stable person in her changing world, was seriously ill:

> I felt closest to God when my father was in the hospital. It was on my birthday when he was admitted into the critical care unit. He lost seven or eight pints of blood due to internal bleeding, because of a tear in his esophagus. He almost died that day. That was when I needed God the most.

Adding to the drama of her potential loss of security, her father became ill on her birthday—a marker of change in a girl's life. She needed God to provide a sense of permanence and to keep her whole when her father was so severely disabled.

* * *

Two younger girls, from Fort Worth, Texas, talked about feeling closest to God when one of their friends died from an allergic reaction to a bee sting. This friend was at school on the playground when she was stung; she died in front of all of her classmates. According to their teachers, this naturally had a huge effect on the other students. Some of them became phobic and refused to go take recess on the playground. Some became withdrawn; some wanted to leave school.

These two girls interpreted their friend's death theologically:

> Jamie (11): *I felt closest to God when my friend Kate died at school. I felt that she had been chosen to be with God and he was telling me that.*

God became close to her, telling her God's secret intentions about her friend. This comforted her, and made her feel better both about the death and about God. It also made her feel more secure in her own faith.

For Christie (12) there was no special revelation, but just a feeling that God was present with her. *I felt close to God when my friend Kate died, because I felt he was helping me get through it.* She felt that God would provide whatever she needed to make it through, despite what her other friends were going through.

When their understanding of the world began to get shaky, as they watched a friend die, unexpectedly, on the playground, God was there as a secure force—explaining and comforting.

* * *

For Amanda (15) from rural Indiana, God's presence in a crisis gives a sense of perspective. She raises sheep and is proud of the animals she cares for. She likes to show them in competition at the Indiana State Fair, but several years ago a disaster struck:

Amanda: *I believe in myself . . . to get through a lot of things that I've done in life . . . my education . . . and I show animals. God helps me a lot too. I show sheep, and he helps me get through those shows. He helps me a lot.*

Q: What kinds of problems do you have showing sheep?

Amanda: *A couple of years ago when a dog got into our lambs' pen and killed a bunch of lambs. God helped me to get through a lot of things. We were getting ready to go to State Fair, and those were the best animals we had. Dogs got in there and killed a couple of ewes and bulls. He helped us a lot with that, too.*

Q: How did God help you with that?

Amanda: *Saying that when you get through it, there'll be other animals there that will be better than those, you know. Things like that. But it still makes you upset.*

She takes pride in her own achievements and has learned to rely on herself. But when the disaster struck, and the dogs killed her lambs, God helped her to understand that she could "get through it." Other animals would come that might be even better. She's not quite sure that she's convinced of that line of comfort; she grieves for the lambs and other animals, and she grieves for the loss of her chance to compete with them.

She acknowledges that the pain is still very real—*it still makes you upset*—but God was with her through the hard times.

* * *

God sometimes allows horrible things to happen in order to allow God's purpose to be fulfilled. Caronda, from South Dallas, talks about an experience of grieving for her cousin:

> *I've had a religious experience. Five months ago the Lord took my cousin to a better place, just one day after she'd given birth to a baby girl. I asked, "Why has God done such an awful thing?" My prayers to God gave me an answer. The answer was, "He did this for the sake of the baby—to make it a better life for this child." Those prayers and answers gave me a better understanding over God and his ways.*

Caronda's understanding encompasses both horror and wonder. God is the central player in all these females' lives. God is serious about a baby's life, and does an "awful thing"—taking Caronda's cousin "to a better place"—in order to protect the baby girl. The juxtaposition of life and death, grief and joy is dramatic in this story. Prayers are answered, and God's will is revealed. There is meaning in tragedy, but God is revealed as one who initiates awful acts in the service of God's plans.

3 ❧

Girls Talk about
Their Churches

In middle school I had a real hard time finding myself and how I wanted other people to perceive me. My so-called friends slowly just started dropping. . . . So I knew that if I could make it through the week I'd be able to come to church and have my friends here at church, even if it was just for two hours on Sunday morning. That was my security blanket, just knowing I could come.

—Susan, 16

I think there are a lot of desperate, hungry people who have been spiritually raped by some charlatan who claims to have the will of God.

—Emily, 17

Nilla was twelve years old, the sister of three older sisters, and the daughter of the most eccentric parents in her rural township. Their gray old house was set back from a dirt road, surrounded by untidy fields. Their barn was teeming with dogs, cats, kittens, baby pigs, a ragged old horse, and assorted wild orphans. Their back woods were rumored to be the site of cult rituals, and Nilla herself said she'd found possible sacrificial remains by the overgrown pond there.

Halloween was the family specialty. Halloween nights Nilla's father became a vampire, and her mother became a hag. The combination of the two monsters and their enthusiasm for their roles scared local trick-or-treaters out of their wits every year. It was a rare child who had the courage to actually accept the candy offered. For several years fundamentalist churches in the area picketed the house in hopes of shutting down the family's extravagant Halloween enterprise. Even without the vampire and witch on the porch, however, the house had a spooky aura. Even their minister tried not to visit at night.

Despite her family's eccentricities, Nilla had many friends. She usually looked and behaved like most of the rest of them— except that she got better grades in school. She was, in most ways, a normal kid with strange tales to tell. She loved to tell her stories: of ghosts in her bedroom, tapping noises in her basement, candles that would burn without having been lit by human hands. Although neither she nor her sisters or parents attended worship regularly, she had a keen interest in traditional Christianity and was a regular attendee at the local Methodist church Sunday school. She was the student who could be depended upon to notice the odd subtexts in the Bible stories and the one who demanded explanations of hard passages.

The year she was in sixth grade, she and her parents decided that it would be a good thing for her to be in the church Christmas Eve pageant being organized by the new pastor's wife. Being sensitive to avoid leaving anyone out, or casting people in roles they didn't want, the pastor's wife was determined to allow the children to choose their own parts. She assigned Mary and Joseph to two older children, then gathered all the others and began slowly to read the familiar story of Jesus' birth. As she read, the children called out the characters they wanted to play; angels, shepherds, kings, lambs, donkeys, camels all claimed their roles. At the end of the story, Nilla hadn't found a role to suit her.

Mrs. Alexander, the costume manager, tried to coax Nilla into being a king or shepherd, to no avail. Nilla finally asked if she could have the Bible. She took it off to read by herself. For fifteen or twenty minutes she was hardly noticed, reading intently, amid all the confusion of trying to find wings and crowns and tails for all the angels, kings, and beasts.

After awhile she returned. "Mrs. Alexander, I've found my role."

"Yes, Nilla—who are you going to be?"

"A hit man."

Mrs. Alexander swallowed hard, noticing the upward glance of the minister's wife. "There are no hit men in this story, honey."

"Right here: 'Rise, take the child and his mother, and flee to Egypt, and remain there till I tell you; for Herod is about to search for the child, to destroy him.' I want to be Herod's hit man."

"What would a hit man wear?"

"All black—to hide—and he'd carry a sword."

"You're sure that's what you want?"

"Yes, ma'am."

"Okay, Nilla. That's you."

On that Christmas Eve night—thanks to Mrs. Alexander and Nilla—their Methodist church saw and heard a fuller version of the story of Christ's birth, with both the wonder and the horror intact. In this church the wise men traveled to King Herod before they arrived in Bethlehem; they were accompanied by a shadowy figure on their way to the stable. Outside the stable, a hit man lurked as Mary cherished the baby and the angels sang. On that Christmas Eve, Nilla's church may have been the only church in Christendom to remember Christ's birth in this more complete narrative, including not only the beauty and glory but also the fear, the evil, the grief, and the hit man.

* * *

Just as a girl's personal relationships with her friends, her family, and God are crucial to her psychological and spiritual well-being, so a positive, trusting, and open relationship with her community of faith is vitally important to her sense of empowerment and belonging in the world. A community becomes, for an adolescent, the forum for testing herself, for learning about personal limits and gifts, and for receiving the affirmation that she is a person of worth and significance, even if, like Nilla, she is in some ways different than most of the other church members or has a very distinctive personal style. Churches that welcome girls (people!) of all kinds are, in turn, enriched in their worship and fellowship experiences and, indeed, even in their understandings of God.

Developmental theorists agree that an adolescent's positive reception into her larger social world plays an enormous role in her development as an adult.[1] As a child develops into a woman, she begins to define herself as a person through her relationships, through her personal decisions and choices, and through an immense amount of inner psychic work. Within family and social spheres the girl must find a new way of being—as one who is not yet an adult in responsibilities and tasks, yet who is no longer a child. She has no more important task than learning where she stands in the eyes of others. Her social world provides her a mirror into which she can gaze, to see how her new image is reflected in others' eyes.

Not all mirrors are equally charitable, however. Many aspects of a girl's culture reflect a distorted image back to her. Powerful social mirrors may seem to show her that she is not "normal" enough, or rich enough, or thin enough, or pretty enough, or smart enough, or (more recently) athletic enough to be successful. Indeed, as will be discussed in chapter 4, some cultural mirrors for adolescent girls are so powerful and so influential that they may altogether prevent girls from seeing themselves through their own eyes.

A girl's faith community should provide relief from the other potentially hazardous mirrors. Her church should reflect her image back to her in a beneficent and generous way. Faith communities should help a girl experience wholeness, feelings of continuity between childhood and adulthood, and feelings of congruity between what she conceives herself to be and what she believes others see in her and expect of her.[2] Churches should be "safe houses" for girls in which their identities and voices are valued and protected.[3]

In return, a girl honors her faith community by recognizing it in her own way—by joining with it through confirmation, by participating in worship, and by adding her voice to others in the community conversation and ongoing life. Erik Erikson writes that, ideally, a community should recognize a young person with "a display of surprise and pleasure in making the acquaintance of a newly emerging individual." Then it should, in turn, should appreciate that it is honored and enriched "by the individual who cares to ask for recognition."[4]

GIRLS APPRECIATE THEIR CHURCHES

Many of the girls who took part in this study felt that their churches were like larger families. They talked about feelings of being safe and happy when they were at church, and they were especially appreciative of any personal or group recognition they received from older adult members. When and where their voices were elicited and heard, the girls were surprised and grateful.

"My Church Is Like My Family"

Girls who love their churches often seem to do so because their congregations treat them like family, and because they feel that their presence makes a difference in their communities. Almost every girl in the study who had positive feelings for her church talked about the ways the church made her feel special and the ways members valued her contributions. Girls appreciate personal warmth among the members. Many feel that their churches care for their entire families along with all the other members—no one is left out. This kind of atmosphere is unique to their churches; their schools, for example, are places where competition is valued over friendships, and rivalry is intense. Church is a place where rivalries are transcended and outside-world "standards" can be relaxed.

> Carrie (16): *I think there are standards, but they're not like totally weird standards—like to look perfect all the time, like not saying the wrong things—I feel like I can be myself at church.*

Sophie (14), Megan (16), and Mollie (17) were interviewed during Sunday school hour at their Methodist church in Colorado.

When they were asked about what they considered to be the best part of their church, they responded with observations about how the people are able relate to one another in positive ways and to accept one another.

Sophie explained that her parents were married at the church many years ago, then stopped attending. They had returned to regular involvement only within the last year:

> Sophie: *One reason we came back to this church was everyone just welcomed us. It was really good, because, you know, everybody wasn't like, "Oh, no, another person's coming in!" They welcomed you, and everybody's really nice and they come down the halls and say "Hi" to you and all. People are really loving here.*

Q: So you didn't feel like an outsider?

> Sophie: *No, it was like we belonged here and came here a long time ago. They just like remembered us. They just let us in.*

> Megan: *I think that too. I think everybody is really close. Everybody in the church is really close.*

> Mollie: *I think the best part is the level of friendships that you have here. It's unconditional love all the time. It never stops . . . it doesn't matter what school you go to. Everybody's just friends and we welcome everybody. And I think that's really cool.*

Q: Is there a lot of rivalry between the high schools?

Megan: (Laughs.) *Yeah!*

Q: But you don't have that here?

Sophie: *No. We all get together like after church, and do things together, and it doesn't matter where you go to school.*

Just as girls value trustworthiness in their relationship to God, they value it in their relationships in the church. For girls, who feel they need to keep secrets to survive, and who construct underground realms in which to live away from the eyes of those who could hurt or devalue them, trust is one of the most important aspects of any relationship. In girl-friendly churches, girls' secrets were held inviolate:

Sophie: *Our church is so open to other people, because the people here trust each other a lot. A lot of people show respect for each other and they . . . people trust each other. If you talk to someone they're going to try to help you. If you ask them, "Please, I just want you to know," they're going to keep it that way. Confidential. So, I think it's just a lot of trust and a lot of love.*

Mollie: *I think it helps, too, that a lot of people know each other. And they do trust each other, because they know each other.*

Connections with Other Worshipers

The interpersonal aspects of community are reflected in various parts of the church's life together. In addition to the importance of personal relationships, many girls value a feeling of connection to other worshipers during services. They want to worship with people they know and trust and who care about them. They love services where their whole families are present; Christmas and Easter are very important for this reason.

Mollie: *Christmas is a time for love. And it's a really happy time for me. And people are more happy and they're excited too, and at least a lot of people are really happy at Christmas. It's a time to feel closer to God or just to remember him, and it's just like a big wake-up and reminder.*

Sophie: *I think Christmas is a time for people who forget what they have with their families. You get closer to your family. Like, I've done it before, forget how close your family is, and that they're there for you and stuff, and then Christmas is a time when you realize what you really have.*

Q: How do you get closer to your family at Christmas?

Sophie: *We all go to church together. Usually we're all here . . . my grandparents too . . . my whole family.*

Some girls who attended small churches mentioned feeling sorry for those who "have to" attend churches that are larger. Girls attending large churches tried to find the family atmosphere in smaller groups, usually in the youth fellowships or "faith-sharing" groups. In either case, if personal connections with the rest of the congregants were not present, girls seemed to lose the sense of God's presence and the feeling of really worshiping.

Janet (15) is from a small rural church:

We went to this big, huge church, and it was so big. There were like TV screens and they like showed the people who'd read the psalm off the TV screen. And you're looking up there and thinking, "What am I doing here?" because it was fake, and I felt like I was just sitting in an auditorium with these other people just singing and it didn't even feel like it had anything to do with God anymore.

Personal connection is also important for Jill (17):

If I stopped going to church I'd miss all the adults. At school there's the teachers, but you can't talk to them the way you can talk to the adults at church. I mean they're like your friends . . .

Moira (16) is from a larger church in the suburbs of Atlanta. She also states that she prefers the smaller gatherings of worshipers that take place infrequently in her congregation:

I like the worships with just the right amount of people so you know mostly everybody, and there's a lot of people, so you know there's more people than just you. But if there's too many people it just doesn't seem like a worship.

Where the people of the church are connected to one another in respectful and loving relationships, where there is acceptance of those with differences, where girls can trust that what they say will be heard, valued, and kept confidential, then girls will be likely to love their communities of faith. Churches that nurture girls are places where they can develop into people of faith along with their families. Where girls feel part of positive and faithful relationships, they feel the presence of God.

Women as Leaders

Girls who love their churches inevitably can name one or two people who represent and exemplify the church's love to them. They were especially appreciative of women who were willing to be models and mentors for them. Girls who were fortunate enough to have a woman pastor or youth group leader were especially grateful for her presence.

For Megan, Mollie, and Sophie, their youth group leader, Joette, was the woman to whom they felt closest:

Q: Whom would you be most likely to go to with a problem?

Megan: *I'd probably go to Jo.*

Mollie: *Because Jo's really trustworthy. It's easy to talk to her because she's female and strong too. She's very trustworthy—you can trust her a lot. She's very open and tries her best to understand us.*

Sophie: *I'd probably go with Jo too. She's very understanding. She'd try to do anything to help you out, you know. I think she would help a lot.*

*   *   *

Katy, Sarah, and Heather, ages 12 and 13, had similar feelings about Angie, their pastor. They were interviewed together after a Sunday night youth-group meeting in Dallas:

Katy: *The best part about my church is my pastor! Angie . . . Angie's the pastor. Did anyone else put the "paz"?*

Sarah: *I put that, the "paz." She has "paz" on her door. Everybody knows she's cool.*

Heather: *She's friendly. She's the first woman we've had, and she understands us. She understands everyone.*

Q: How do you know she understands you?

Katy: *She helps us—she teaches us—and she can help us with problems. Like when there's something at school that we want to tell her about she always listens to us.*

The girls speak all at once—all agreeing with this.

Sarah: *She always wants to hear our problems.*

Heather: *But not during serious times, like confirmation class. But during youth groups and "snack time."*

Katy: *You know the question [on the questionnaire] about who affects your faith the most, well, I put Angie for that too.*

Q: How does she help your faith?

Katy: *She helps me understand about whatever . . . like, if you don't understand something, she can always tell you if you don't understand it.*

Sarah: *She makes it funner than just teaching out of the Bible, and it could be really boring and everything, but she makes everything into a game. And it makes it easier to learn.*

Clarisse (16), Cherie (16), and Hattie (15) from a large church in Indianapolis, have a special relationship with their youth leader, Marina. They are dancers; Marina instructs them and encourages them to use dance in worship. She also has taught the church the importance of allowing the girls to perform:

Clarisse: *If there is one person who really influences my faith it would be Marina. She's not a pastor; she's my youth leader. She shares the love of the arts with me. She lives through God, and she's helped me through life—becoming more involved through the church and making me feel welcome.*

Cherie: *What I like about this church is that they accept different things that a more traditional church doesn't. At my old church they wouldn't let something like dance in the worship, but here, you know, it's very—they try to use the youth and the kids a lot. That helps us relate to God.*

Hattie: *I like the opportunities to dance that you wouldn't necessarily get at another church, because I dance myself. I moved here about five years ago, and I hadn't had any experience with dance in the church up to that point. And so it gave me a new perception on how to worship.*

Q: And Marina is your leader for that?

Hattie: *Yeah, she helped me do a lot of stuff with the kids here. Like I choreographed a musical. That was last week. And Julie is another person who dances in the church, and she's helped us work on dancing at Christmas.*

Marina has had tremendous influence on the girls, not only in coaching them in dancing but also in making a space for them in the church's worship. In doing this, she has taught them a profound spiritual lesson—it is possible to be a girl and to do important things in the service of God.

Clarisse: *My favorite way to worship would probably be dancing. Because it's what I do best. I guess everybody has like a personal talent, and that's my talent and I love doing it. And I like the fact that I can do my favorite thing in the world and also worship God at the same time.*

* * *

Girls in a dance troupe in an African American church in south Dallas also named their female pastor as the person most influential to their faith. They spoke less in terms of a personal relationship with this woman—their dance coaches were other women and men in the church—and more about their respect for her. It is clear that Rev. Pattison holds a position of great power in their community. They are especially grateful for the time she takes for them and for her explanations of the Bible in their own language. In their minds no one else could help them in this way:

De Andree (13): *She clearly states what is going on in the Bible, and when we need help she makes it better to understand, which allows me to understand more.*

Vanesia (15): *She explains the Bible to us in words we can understand. She breaks it down into modern-day terms, where we can say, "Oh, okay." She always says that everything's that happening now happened in the Bible. She just refers it back to what's happening now, and looks like, "We understand—we understand how that works." So Rev. Pattison is most important to me also.*

Kim (14): *She's open and she helps us understand things that we might not understand, and no one else could help us understand.*

When these girls were asked what they *disliked* most about their religion, they agreed that the worst thing about being Methodist was that their minister could be taken away from them any year:

Kim: *Every Methodist church, if you get close to the pastor, then they have to move on to different churches. I've been through three or four pastors here at this church, and it hurts when the pastor has to leave when you're close to them.*

* * *

Women who take the time to be models and mentors for girls contribute greatly to their spiritual nurture. Girls talk about being understood by these women and, in turn, being taught by them in ways that others couldn't. They are grateful for women they can trust with their problems. They are appreciative of women who are female and strong, women who help them with their problems, but also require them to be serious and to learn about their faith. These women connect the girls with the church, make spaces for them, and give them skills for worship. These women make learning fun and teach the Bible in ways that connect with girls' lives so they can "understand how [faith] works."

Participating in Worship

The girls in this study especially like forms of worship in which they can actively participate. As shown above, the girls who were coached in liturgical dance and then allowed to dance in worship services felt honored and connected to God and the community. In other, more regular, worship services girls tended to enjoy the singing most, especially singing hymns with updated melodies and lyrics. Even girls who felt that worship services in general were boring admitted to enjoying singing with their congregations.

Caroline (15), Kami (14), and Jen (15) are from a rural Presbyterian church:

Caroline: *I like the service when pretty much all they do is sing songs, 'cause I really like the songs. I can't sing, but I like to listen to other people.*

Kami: *Yeah, I like it when you can call out a number that you want to sing, but they don't do that very often. They do it like at Christmas.*

Jen: *I like the newer songs, not like the old boring ones that most churches sing. I like the newer songs . . . more upbeat, faster, better.*

Kami: *But that's the opposite of me, because I like the older ones.*

Caroline: *I like music better than listening to people, because my mind wanders too much when people talk. Like I find myself thinking, like, what I'm going to wear and . . . (Laughs.) I like music . . . any kind. Singing, bells, or anything.*

Sermons

While music seemed to be the favorite part of the worship service for most girls, other aspects of worship left girls bored or confused. Sermons seemed to be the most alienating aspect of church for girls; most were not interested in or had very negative feelings about sermons. Several complained that they could not focus their attention on them; most girls seemed to feel that the sermon had almost nothing to do with their lives. For several, the sermon was clearly an aspect of worship they dreaded.

One Presbyterian girl tried to stay away from worship as much as possible because she resented the preacher telling her from on high what should be important in her life:

I don't like listening to somebody who I don't really like that much preach at me from the pulpit up there, telling me some story from the Bible and how it relates to life . . . because when I listen to him, it doesn't really relate to me.

A Roman Catholic college student from Philadelphia felt free to tell me that she hated church authorities and felt repulsed by their sermons on women and birth control. She talked about feelings of helplessness as she listened to her preacher, knowing that he was reflecting official church teachings; she wondered how she could remain part of a church that didn't share her values.[5]

Most girls, Protestant and Catholic, did not have such strong feelings about church teachings and sermons. Many, however, admitted to feeling disconnected with the church during sermons. Their concerns were not addressed; youth were often spoken of in stereotypical ways; the language used was foreign to their experience. Girls' resistance to sermons could be interpreted as resistance to those elements of worship that silenced them.

Sacraments

Many girls also admitted feeling confused about participating in the sacraments. Most expressed the feeling that they didn't understand what was happening during the rituals of their churches very well. For some that meant that the rituals weren't meaningful. Katherine (15), a Presbyterian, blames herself for not feeling moved by communion:

> Personally, this may not be right, but I really don't get much out of communion. I don't know what my problem is, but I can't get much feeling out of it. . . . I don't know. . . . You're just sitting there. And like they pass bread around and they don't even say anything about it. This is the cup, or this is the blood of Christ. Let's drink it together. This is the body, and we'll eat it, and then that's the extent of it.

She worries about the children in the congregation who seem to act like it's a game:

> I see these little kids, they pick up the bread and then they drop it on the floor. They think it's food; they don't understand why, and I don't think it's right for these little kids. It's almost like mocking it, but in a way I don't understand it either.

Other girls in her church feel differently about communion. They talk about liking to take communion when they were little, because it was something they could *do* during the service. Now that they have been confirmed and had some teaching about it, they feel more confident about participating.

> Caroline (15): *When we were really little my Mom wouldn't let me do it, because we didn't really understand why, and then, I don't know, it was a while ago and she let us do it then. And after confirmation I really understood what it was about. So then it felt more meaningful than just eating a piece of bread. Because when I was little I saw my Mom eating bread and I didn't really understand why I couldn't, because I wanted some. And the little cups, I liked that.*

> Sally (14): *Yeah, when I was little I remember it was just something cool, because I never got anything out of worship. And the bread was like yes!, you know? Something for me! This is cool. And after confirmation you actually realize what it was for.*

Janet (17) has a more mystical view of communion than her friends. She feels connected to the historical Jesus through the physical acts of eating and drinking:

> *I like getting communion, because it makes me think that this was what Jesus was doing a long time ago. And I just think it's really neat how it's still going on, and that it's lasted this long. So it must be really important. . . . We don't have many connections with Jesus because it's so long ago. I mean, not real connections, like physical connections. This is one of them, like that he did it and now we do it. It's the same thing.*

Youth Services

In churches where youth participate regularly in worship, girls spoke about how meaningful it was to be an acolyte, to read the Scriptures, and to lead the congregation in prayer. In churches with traditions of annual youth services, every girl who participated expressed excitement about the chance to lead worship for the adults in the congregation. Even girls who were going through periods of questioning the church and God seemed to find real meaning in youth services.

Desa (13), Rachel (13), and Ali (12) were interviewed in their church "attic" on the evening after the Youth Sunday in which they had all participated. Although there was disagreement among them about which part was the most fun, which parts were corny, and who should get credit for what, they all were so excited about the day's activities that they could barely stay seated:

Rachel: *I think that every Sunday should be Youth Sunday. That was fun. It made it go by really fast. And something else: we had three people join at the end! And we were really good!*

Desa: *Yeah, the congregation felt like they could talk to us . . . the congregation was more open this time, to us.*

Q: Tell me your favorite part of what you did today.

Desa: *Um, mostly all of it, but really that we got to be in charge, and also I liked that part at the beginning when me and James invited everyone to worship, but it was kind of corny.*

Ali: *It was corny!*

Desa: *We got to run around the church and say, "It's time for worship! Where are you guys? It's time for worship!"*

Ali: *We were all hiding.*

Desa: *I also liked the part where we did the skits. In the sermon.*

Ali: *My favorite part was when the choir sang. I'm in the choir.*

Rachel: *And I liked the dance. . . . First Alice would dance, and then it was Alice and Kati, and then all the rest of us . . . and it was fun. It was a song called, "I Believe in God." You can hear it and we'll dance it for you! (At this point all the girls got up and danced for several minutes.)*

Desa: *Annie's good. She choreographed it. She's in ninth grade. She choreographed every bit of it.*

Q: Okay, and . . .

Desa: *No, no. I'm not done! And, um, the skits. I liked the skits and I liked the prayers of the people that I did. It was fun. I made people cry!*

Rachel: *You did?!?!*

Desa: *Yeah, I made your Dad cry. He told my mom that. He told my mom.*

Ali: *On which one?*

Desa: *The prayer that I did . . . "Dear God."*

Rachel: *You didn't even make that prayer.*

Desa: *I know.*

Rachel: *She just read it off a piece of paper.*

Desa: *But your dad told my mom that he saw a side of me he'd never seen before, which I don't know is good or bad.*

Rachel: *Can I go to the bathroom?*

The adrenaline was still very much in evidence seven hours later. The girls were impressed with themselves and their abilities. They were also still learning about what had transpired during the service—giving each other feedback, not letting anyone claim too much credit, happy to think that people would listen to them, and especially pleased that three people had joined the church because of them. Rachel was clearly miffed to find out that her father cried at Desa's prayer, but the overall mood was extremely positive. They felt very good about one another and good about the church. They felt they had made a real contribution to worship. Later they remarked that they hoped the little children of the church had enjoyed it; they were happy to be part of a youth tradition and wanted younger children to look forward to following in their footsteps.

* * *

Two older girls from a Denver Presbyterian church were more circumspect about their Youth Sunday. But they clearly liked being able to talk to the church and share some of their kind of music—even though it had to be toned down—with the congregation. Up to this point in her interview Courtney had not been able to think of anything that she liked about worship at any time of year; she finally remembered the youth choir on Youth Sunday:

> Courtney: *I don't like being up in front of people, so I kind of avoid it. Except I'm in the choir, and that's fun.*

> Sarah: *I like being the center of attention, so I really love it. Youth Sunday is a Sunday where we plan the whole service, and then we do the whole service. I did the Word to the Children, so that was fun.*

> Q: What was the best part of that service?

> Courtney: *The fact that it shows that we can do something too. You know, and it's a little different. We still have to follow some rules, but it's different and that's nice. We get to choose the music. Usually like the youth choir isn't as up-to-date as what's on the radio, but you can't really play that in a church service, so . . . but we sang a song one year that I really loved.*

Girls who participate in youth services often seem almost shocked that their churches allow them this time. They talk about feeling that, on most Sundays, there are separations between teenagers and older people in the church; they feel that some older people think teenagers aren't able to do or be much good. The youth service is a time to show the church that they are responsible, decent, and creative; and it is a time to give their best efforts as a contribution to the community's life. They feel honored to be given the chance, and they feel proud when adults listen to them.

GIRLS' DISSATISFACTION
WITH THEIR CHURCHES

Some of the girls who expressed deep appreciation for their churches *also* had serious criticisms; other girls were *only* critical. Most of the girls' criticisms stemmed from three issues: (1) a perceived lack of integrity between what adults teach about their faith and how they actually behave, (2) a perceived lack of honest wrestling with controversial issues, especially relating to sexuality and the treatment of gay and lesbian people, and (3) the perception that the church and/or their parents are forcing them to accept faith on terms other than their own.

When the Church Lacks Integrity of Belief and Action

Adolescence can be a crucial time for the development of personal faith. Developmental theorists such as James Fowler[6] and Sharon Parks[7] describe late adolescence, especially, as being a time when young adults have the mental capacities to begin to graduate from mere acceptance of their churches' and families' faith to a formulation of faith that more nearly fits their own beliefs and experiences. This more authentic personal faith is usually based in church and family traditions but is willing to test the limits, ask questions, probe, and ultimately to reject those aspects that are perceived as unsatisfactory or inconsistent.

During adolescence girls watch their churches and families more closely than ever, as they begin the process of sorting through, testing, and working out their own personal faith commitments. Just as relationships are crucial in other areas of girls' lives, relationships are critical for their faith development. Girls pay special attention to the ways faith influences relationships—does it lead to fairness and reciprocity? promote honesty? enable forgiveness? help when you're worrying over everyday problems? help one to face hard issues?

For girls' sakes, adults need to be careful that their teaching, their actions, and their relationships reflect a deep integrity—

that their own faith stances are consistent with the actions they take, the decisions they make, and the ways in which they maintain relationships. Girls tend to judge the church most harshly when church leaders don't live up to the girls' standards of integrity, when relationships are troubled by persistent conflict, and when official proclamations are in tension with girls' own beliefs or experiences. Specific complaints about lack of integrity or courage tend to be connected to the issues most important and controversial to the adults in their communities. Not surprisingly, these include money, power, and sexuality.

Especially in rural churches, where families seemed to be less affluent, the issue of money and how the church deals with it weighs heavily on girls' minds. When Megan, Mollie, and Sophie were asked to describe the biggest problem in their church, they talked about the church's problems with money and how it affected their worship, their families, and their faith.

Megan: *In the worship service they talk about money a lot. It becomes a big issue, you know, especially to be really worried about it. I don't think the church really has money problems, but it's just that they worry about how much people are going to give to the church.*

Mollie: *I think the church is starting to become—I can't think of the word for it—it's just starting to become more of a money issue. It's not just some of the people talking about it. My parents, every week, they make sure they write a check. I think everyone's saying: "Let's see, how much should I give?" And there are weeks when they can't afford it, but we still do it. I think the church worries too much about that.*

Q: So people are just a little too nervous?

Mollie: *Yeah. I think the people that go to this church are loyal, and they want to make sure that the church is alive. And if we got some money problems, they'd be there. I don't think we have to worry at all.*

The girls feel that the church is taking the wrong attitude toward stewardship. For church leadership to be worried about money reveals a lack of confidence in God and in the community. For these girls, it is especially hard to hear about money problems in the worship service. The effects of worrying have spilled over into their family relationships:

Megan: *That's what my Dad has been saying, too. . . . And [my parents] fight about it. My mom will be down and thinks about how much money they should give and that they can't afford it. So they only give, you know, like just a little bit. I think my parents shouldn't have to worry about the money deal, I mean, to have to talk about that, because, you know . . . God will take care of it. They don't have to talk about it, 'cause he'll take care of it for them. I don't think they need to worry about it.*

Q: Do you believe that God takes care of money in your family?

Megan: *He helps us, like, he doesn't take care of it for us, but it's like he's there when we need the help of getting through it.*

The girls' theology about money is rooted in their own experience of going through hard times. They don't expect that God will give them miracle money to pay their bills or make it easy for them to buy luxury items, but they all have experienced God's presence in the middle of financial hardships. God helps them to maintain a sense of dignity and honor even when they feel poor:

Mollie: *Things are kind of tight in our family, because my mom had surgery, and she's not working. But it's not like God says, "Okay, you guys can win the lottery right now, because you need money." I think he helps us realize that things like honor are important. But there's not going to be this . . . nothing bad's going to happen to us, things will just be a little tight for now, and that's it.*

Sophie: *That's how it is with us too. A couple of years we were tight with money, and we couldn't buy things. He helped us through it. I mean he doesn't tell us, "Okay, you're going to win the lottery now—go out and get a lottery ticket and you're going to win a million dollars." He doesn't do it, you know. I mean he'll tell us, "You're okay—you'll make it through." And we did. You know, you just can't say that he's going to give you the money. He'll guide you through it, though.*

Megan: *Yeah, it's not like money growing on trees and you can just pick it off and pay your bills off or whatever.*

They don't understand why their parents and the church can't face up to money hardships or why they seem to need to discuss money all the time. Their own experience has taught them that even if the family loses a significant part of their income, they survive. God doesn't offer winning lottery tickets or money trees, but God did not desert them. God kept them focused on more important things. God can be trusted to "guide you through." Worrying about money is destructive of family life and causes unnecessary arguments and problems between their parents. More importantly for the girls, however, it seems to be an act of distrust or unfaith to provoke worry about money during a worship service. This is, as far as they are concerned, the worst problem in their church.

When the Church Refuses to Answer Questions

Girls have a strong desire to learn as much truth as they can about issues of importance to them, even though they are often hesitant to ask questions loudly or persistently. When they work up courage to ask questions, they resent it when adults sidestep or avoid answering them. As we saw in chapter 2, girls view honest and open communication as integral to being in relationship. People in relationships listen to each other, respond to each other's needs, and speak truthfully about all important issues. If girls show the courage to ask hard questions, they want adults to reciprocate with hard answers.

In chapters 4 and 5 girls talk about their churches' failure to take the girls' questions about sexuality and violence seriously enough and about the impact that neglect has on their faith. In this section we look at the girls' struggle to understand why their parents and other church leaders won't address the issue of gay and lesbian rights and the church. This is an important issue for the girls in itself, but it is also illustrative of other controversial issue that the girls wished would be talked about openly in church. It was especially on the Colorado girls' minds in the years I interviewed them, because of the very recent referendum in Colorado deciding whether gays and lesbians should legally be protected from discrimination.

The girls had two complaints about how the church handled the issue: (1) they felt uneasy that the adult members of the church wouldn't talk about the issue, and (2) they saw not talking as a matter of basic mistrust and fear.

Q: At my place of worship, we rarely talk about . . . ?

Katherine (15): *There's actually two things. One of them is gay rights and the second is that God can be a man and a woman.*

Of the two issues, the second—the gender of God—is dropped immediately in favor of discussing the first. Girls talked a bit about God and gender later, but it turned out mainly to be Katherine's concern.

Caroline (15): *I agree with Katherine about gay people. Because the people in the church are totally afraid of that, and they don't want to take a stand on anything, because they're afraid to offend people. I really feel like that. They don't talk about that sort of thing. They talk about pretty much else, but when it comes to gay people and—*

Q: They can talk about AIDS and sex and drugs and alcohol, but not gay people?

Several girls speaking at once: *Yeah—any other thing.*

Caroline: *It's just like . . . I don't think our church really wants to take a stand on it . . . is what I feel. Because they never said it; they never said it's wrong. I mean they don't come out and say it's wrong. And I think they should say it's wrong.*

Caroline takes a stand: Being gay is wrong, and church leaders should come out and say that. She feels that everyone should feel the same way, and for the leaders to resist saying it is cowardice.

Katherine: *I guess it's because people think it's nonexistent.*

Q: That there aren't gay people here?

Katherine: *Yeah, that it's just not a part of this community. They just live elsewhere.*

Q: And you feel that there *are* gay people in this community?

Katherine: *Yes. . . . [The people in the church] don't really talk about what they truly believe in. They think, like "go with the flow" sometimes, but they really don't say what they believe in.*

Katherine doesn't agree with Caroline, but she doesn't attack her views directly. She feels that the issue isn't spoken of because adults don't realize that the issue affects their community also—there are gay and lesbian people living in the community. Also, it's easier not to make waves in the community—easier to go with the flow—ignoring the issue.

Caroline: *I think they avoid it, things staring them in the face. They avoid it because they really don't know what to say. And I think everybody does that because they just really don't want to take a stand.*

Caroline returns to her issue in a new way. The other girls didn't agree with her assessment that being gay or lesbian is wrong, so she backs off her initial statement. Rather, she tries to explain the lack of attention to an important issue as a matter of being unsure—"they don't know what to say."

Q: Is that a big fear?

Janet (17): *I think it is, because they want to be politically right, and they don't want to be judged by other people.*

Sally (14): *I think they don't want to say anything that they think is different from what anybody else believes, because they don't want to be different or judged, or thought of differently, you know?*

Caroline: *I agree that some people don't say what they believe in really, because they don't want to be judged, and they may be afraid that they're wrong.*

Caroline, reassured by two other voices affirming her assessment, joins back in the conversation on the issue of judgment. No one wants to be judged for holding the wrong beliefs on an important issue, especially when one isn't sure if he or she is correct. And no one wants to be thought of as being different.

Q: People wouldn't talk about it because they really don't know what they believe?

Sally: *I think they don't talk about it because they don't know what to believe. Like whether it's right to be gay or maybe wrong like . . . yeah.*

Q: So, they might say it's right and it's really wrong? Or say it's wrong and it's really right, and they don't want to risk it?

Sally: *Yeah, they don't know what God expects them to think about it so they don't say anything.*

Whether gays and lesbians should receive protection from discrimination has been the focus of national media attention, and it has been an extremely important topic in the girls' schools. They also talk about it at home. The girls have accounted for the adults' silence in the church in various ways:

- Adults are afraid to take a stand, because of fear of offending others.
- They don't understand the situation fully—believing (falsely) that there are no gay or lesbian people in the community.

- They don't know what they believe in and are content to go with the flow.
- They don't know what to say about what they believe.
- They want to be politically right, in order not to be judged by others.
- They don't want to be thought different.
- They may be afraid that they're wrong.
- They don't know what God wants them to think.

For the girls there are many good reasons not to talk, but none of them are adequate. In the entire two-hour interview, this topic elicited the most energy and the most negative feelings toward the church. For the girls, an issue like this should be discussed, no matter what the cost. They admit, however, that they haven't spoken about it in their youth group either. They begin to talk indirectly with each other about what they believe and the advantages of being honest:

Q: Do you talk about it in your youth group?

Caroline: *No, we've never . . . have even like gotten . . . we haven't really gone deep into any sort of subject like this. We just go out and have a good time.*

Janet: *But I think we should. Like all we do is have fun. I mean we should do more of that kind of thing.*

Q: To help you know what you think about things?

Janet: *To talk about it.*

Caroline: *I think you just need to see what other people think, 'cause you really don't know anyone. I feel like I know people, and now I don't know what they believe, and what they feel about certain things. I think it would be really neat to see what they really, truly think.*

They come to a point where it feels safe enough to talk; Janet encourages the rest. For Caroline, if you don't talk about what you believe on the hard issues, you don't really know each other.

Q: If you believe that gays should have all the rights that everybody else has, would that be a dangerous thing to say in your youth group?

Caroline: *No, I think we're pretty much on the same track, because we go to church. I just think most of our youth group would agree with that, that gay people shouldn't get special rights, but that they should get the same rights. They shouldn't get anything special. I think that would pretty much go over.*

The other girls quickly and vigorously express assent with nodding and "yeahs." A consensus has been quickly reached.

Over the course of the discussion, Caroline, who was most willing to state her opinion, has allowed her ideas to be shaped by the other girls. When she stated that "[being gay] is wrong" she was responded to with subtle pressure from the other girls. No one said she was incorrect, but no one agreed with her. She then began to test other ideas "[people] may be afraid they're wrong [in their ideas about gays and lesbians]." Finally, she was able to proclaim a new, more nuanced idea: "[gay people] shouldn't get special rights, but . . . they should get the same rights." By the time she reached her final conclusion, she was expressing the feelings of the group.

Sally: *I think our youth group has a lot of the same ideas and we're open to new ideas and everything, and we won't say: "Oh well, you think that and I don't like you anymore." So you would trust each other enough to be able to say what you really think.*

Janet: *I think we know each other well enough that if they did think otherwise, we would still like them, because we like them for what they are, you know.*

After hearing themselves discuss the issue, the girls feel that their youth group is probably of one mind. There was a sense of relief in the room. There also was an admission that, even if someone disagreed, they would not be outcast: "we like them for what they are . . ."

They had also discovered three more things about themselves: (1) that they could talk together and come to an agreement on an important and potentially divisive issue and (2) that the cohesion of the group was stronger than theoretical disagreements. They had also learned, however, (3) that there would be subtle pressure to conform to a group decision. Caroline's wish to know what everybody "really, truly thinks" could probably not be fulfilled, because of the potential for conflict.

Throughout the discussion they experienced themselves as more courageous than the leaders and other adults of the church. Unlike the adults, they took risks to talk about a confusing and controversial issue about which they might be wrong. They took risks of being judged by one another, paying close attention to one another's expressions of approval and disapproval. Caroline was even willing to take the risk of offending others to begin the discussion. They found that the adults' reasons for not speaking did not excuse them from taking risks. These girls came to a group decision without the help or guidance of the church.

When the Church Gives Too Many Answers

Sele (17) is Baptist by birth and an independent thinker when she's outside her church and family. She struggles with the problem of how to find the religion that corresponds to her ways of thinking while not losing her religious roots:

> You know I'm Baptist. I almost, in a way, wish that I wasn't born a Baptist. I was born Baptist and raised Baptist, and that's the religion I'm in. But I almost wish in a sense that I was given the opportunity to choose a religion.

She feels conflicted; she is grateful that she had religious training and upbringing, but she wishes she had been exposed to more of a range of beliefs and religious experiences:

I think, though, in a way it's not helpful [to be given a choice about religions]. You get to a point when you're old enough to choose, and you're not really interested, you know. I know people that have grown up without religion, and I can't imagine that. So I'm grateful that, you know, not so much that I was born a Baptist, but that I was brought up with a faith as opposed to not having anything. But I'd really like to have an experience of different religions to really decide, you know, which one I'd choose.

Q: Does another type of spirituality or religion appeal to you?

Well, I went to a Quaker camp, and then I did a paper last semester on Quakers. I went to a Quaker meeting, and I used to go to Quaker meetings all the time. When I was at this camp I always thought it was so interesting, but it used to drive my mother crazy that I would come home, and all I would talk about was Quakers. And my father was like, "How can you go there?" My father can't understand how you could sit and just sense and feel Christ.

Sele is deeply impressed by Quaker worship but isn't sure that is the proper mode of religious expression for her. Her quest is to find the right religion for herself, and her disappointment with her family and the Baptist church is that they didn't leave room for exploration: *I don't know that I would choose Quakers, but I know I think it's important to experience different religions.*

Ellie (18) feels more strongly resentful of her religious roots than does Sele. She disagrees with almost everything her priest preaches, and she feels manipulated by him. She believes that her church leaders cater to the "rich elderly parishioners" and don't care about "young people, women, or the poor": *They rarely talk about anything except abortion, why women shouldn't be priests, or why everyone should be a Republican, because of the abortion thing.*

Church leaders seem to be unwilling to allow parish members to think for themselves: *The priests just want everyone to believe what they tell them to believe.* She honors her own abilities to think about theological issues and wants those abilities to be respected.

She is, however, especially grateful for a nun who was a teacher in high school and who allowed her *to make [her] own decisions.* She also highly valued a religious retreat she attended during her senior year in high school because the leaders authorized her questioning and made space for everyone else to begin to think for themselves about important issues:

> *It was the most important religious experience I have ever had. The people didn't try to force religion or faith down my throat like in my parish and in grade school, where they would say, "You have to believe this, and you have to believe that." It was a warm friendly group of people—you could talk without worrying about being laughed at or made fun of.*

Margaret (18) also is dissatisfied with her church because of doctrines with which she disagrees, especially regarding women being priests and priests not being allowed to marry. Her problems with the church have put her into direct and hard conflict with her family, especially with her mother:

> *I think it's because I'm Roman Catholic, and I've talked about this with my mom, and I'm not even sure I want to be Roman Catholic anymore. I think that . . . my mother keeps saying that Roman Catholicism is the only true religion, because it's based on the Bible, and all these other religions were started by outsiders. But the one thing I've learned from God is that you're supposed to love each other, and love everyone, and treat everyone like you'd like to be treated. And I just don't see how the Catholic church says that women can't be priests and priests can't be married, when [loving] is one of the most important commandments. And it's such a paradox that the Roman Catholic Church says that no, you can't be married . . . it's so ridiculous.*

Margaret's own theology and experience of God leads her to oppose her church, her mother, and her mother's interpretation of the Bible. According to her theology, love is the principle that matters above all else, and the church and her family are wrong.

And women can't be priests. I mean, what's wrong with us? The first people that saw Jesus after he resurrected were women, they weren't the disciples, they were women. And to say that women aren't capable of being priests is just ridiculous. I get really upset when I go home, and go to my church at home, because every Sunday they talk about abortion—the priest is able to slip in—something about abortion and how wrong it is, and premarital sex and how you shouldn't have it. And I just sit there, and I get so mad, and I don't think that it's right for the church—I think they can have views and say them— but for them to expect people to . . . It's like they're living in this bubble. When the Pope went to Latin America and told them not to use contraception, I mean, that's just ridiculous! It's just not realistic.

She judges the church by her own experience and her own reading of the Bible. Women were the first to see Jesus, so they should be priests. In her eyes, the church is wrong to expect people to live by its standards on abortion, premarital sex, and contraceptives. Priests can *preach* about these things but shouldn't abuse their power by slipping their views into every sermon. Mainly, the church should move outside the bubble in which it operates and which keeps it out of touch with real life. She doesn't have high hopes that the church will change, unless something drastic happens:

I do think that there will come a time when things will change, but it's really slow. It wasn't until the Black Plague when scientists went to the Pope and said, "Please, we need to dissect a body to figure this out," that he changed that rule that live bodies could be dissected. And that was when there was a huge plague going on.

She wonders about her own future in the Roman Catholic Church—whether for the sake of her relationships with her family she should stay. But she resists the trade-offs involved in staying, including feeling that she is participating in an institution that has lost God's favor:

I think once I go to college, I might change religions. I mean, I say that, but my grandmother would have a heart attack and my mother would disown me, so . . . I think maybe. My mom keeps saying to me that I don't have to believe everything that the church says—that you can still be Roman Catholic and believe other things. But I think the Roman Catholic Church has strayed away from what God wanted and has lost sight of the whole big picture. Why should I go to church and only listen to men preach the sermons when you can learn just as much from women?

So I think there will come a point in my life when I'm going to have to say to my mom, "Look, this is who I am, and this is what I'm going to do. I'm still very religious; you've taught me about God; you've given me a close relationship with God. But I feel the Roman Catholic Church is not the place for me." She'll hopefully just have to deal with it, hopefully.

When she's asked about how she came to think about God in a new way, different than her family's views, she surprisingly credits her mother:

My mother has always been a very independent woman. She was the first woman to go through the XX Corp. management program ever, and she was the Brownie leader once when I was little, and she was the only mom who worked, and she bought the cookies instead of baking them. She was a very progressive mother, and I saw that as I was growing up. She's always challenged people, and we go into stores . . . and she's always assertive. She wants equality, and I just think that I just sort of inherently got that same sort of spirit from her.

Her mother taught her to be independent and to have a courageous spirit. Ironically, Margaret's independence leads her away from the church—the one area of her life in which her mother seems to be traditional and conservative. Margaret believes she will be able to risk her relationship with her mother and grandmother when she is older and *more on [her] own.* Until then she lives in the tension of holding strong beliefs that put her in conflict with the people who are most important to her. She's not ready to reject anything totally yet.

* * *

Girls who are angry at their churches often express the feeling that they are being forced to believe or act in ways that don't make sense to them. Margaret, the most critical of the three, talks about the church's prerogative to *have views and say them.* She does not want to be *forced* to believe everything that the church believes, however. Her mother, apparently, has made a compromise, saying "you don't have to believe everything that the church says—that you can still be Roman Catholic and believe other things." Margaret wonders whether this can be true; she wonders if the church still reflects God's purposes.

Ellie wonders about the politics of religious belief and feels that the necessity to take care of the elderly rich should not take precedence over the need to care for the young, for women, and for the poor. She is especially outraged that her church would try to force a political agenda on its parishioners. She and Sele both resent being told what they have to believe. They are beginning to trust their own theological judgments over those of church leaders and their families, but all are reluctant to push their own beliefs to the point of damaging important relationships. They all feel resentful that they have to make a choice.

4 ✐

Girls Talk about Sexuality and Their Bodies

I'm o.k.
If you get me at a good angle
you're o.k.
In this sort of light
and we don't look
like pages from a magazine
but that's all right
that's all right

> —from "Imperfectly" by Ani DiFranco

I arrived a few minutes late, tossed my Bible and some hand-outs on the table, apologized to the unusually large class, and began the checking-in process that was part of our weekly Sunday school ritual.

"So, how was your week, Andy?"

"Okay."

"Melissa?"

"It was all right."

"Jan?"

"Yeah, Okay."

These were normally talkative kids. I knew something was amiss. There was too much energy in the room for this little chatter.

"All right, what's going on?"

Long silence.

"Does *anyone* want to tell me how their week went?"

Shuffling, no talking.

"Let's start the lesson then. Today we're going to discuss Moses and the burning bush. Let's turn to Exodus."

No movement.

Silence.

"Jan, *what* is going on here?!?"

"Ms. Davis, you said we were going to talk about sex today."

I remembered last week's promise—"Oh my gosh, I totally forgot. Let's do the burning bush this week, and next week I'll be better prepared."

"No," insisted Jake, "Let's talk about it today."

* * *

For adolescents, sexuality is a matter that will not wait. Although it is one of the most politically dangerous issues in today's churches, teenagers want and need truthful information and guidance on this subject. They also want and need forums for discussions about all aspects of sexual behavior and themselves as sexual beings.

This should not surprise us. Most adults remember sexuality and sexual questions being high on our own list of concerns as adolescents, whether or not we were sexually active. Seminary students, adult participants in sexuality education, and other adults with whom I talk about adolescent sexuality have confirmed to me over and over that the church, their teachers, and their parents did miserable jobs of teaching them, as children and adolescents, about sexuality. This is true for my parents' generation, for my generation, and for the generations that have followed. As adolescents, we looked in vain for information on sexuality that had any connection to our own feelings and experiences. Trying to connect that sparse and often incorrect information with our *religious* ideas and values was almost impossible.

Most adults tell me that when they were teenagers they mostly heard about guilt, shame, and hands falling off, or they heard nothing at all from their churches. Most of us would have liked better and more information. The guilt and the silence were devastating.

Like many adult women, my friends and I have memories from adolescence (in the late 1960s) of trying to piece together images and ideas about sex and sexuality from health class scare films (Who can forget the image of the forlorn girl limping down the road at night, abandoned after her first sexual encounter?); the Ten Commandments (Did adultery apply to us? What in the world did "lusting after" mean?); and the little brochures we girls got on menstruation with titles like "Very Personally Yours" and "You're a Young Lady Now."[1] We struggled to decide what "fornication" meant; we were all mystified by the Song of Solomon—how did that relate to *our* boyfriends? We learned about seducing men, and the power of the seductress, by sneaking to movies like *The Valley of the Dolls*.

Even as we experimented with sexuality in our own lives, we learned about its negative effects for girls—diseases, pregnancy, and abuse. We also learned about the culture's values for us—we were to be the gatekeepers, the "no" sayers, the virginity savers. Girls' sexuality, more than boys', was viewed as dangerous and forbidden. We wondered what God thought about us and our sexuality.

In her book *Promiscuities*, Naomi Wolf describes the same sort of hit-or-miss education in sexuality for her generation (adolescents in the 1970s). She writes of combing through *Seventeen* magazine, *Penthouse*, Archie comics, *The Sensuous Woman*, and *Our Bodies, Ourselves* to gain bits of information. Along with the negative messages, her generation was taught that women should be free—by right and by technology—to experience sexuality as men always had:

We as teenagers were meant to believe that the sexual pop culture we saw everywhere around us—from *Penthouse* and *Story of O* to rape fantasies, miniskirts, and the Pill, from *Playboy*'s subsidy of abortion-rights organizations to sex-toy parties for suburban homemakers—was all supposed to be the manifestation of women's sexual freedom.[2]

Although the culture at the time of Wolf's adolescence was more open to discussing sex and sexuality, the topic was no less confusing. There were few adults to ask who were not as baffled as the girls. There were no ready sources of information about what religious belief had to do with one's body, one's development into womanhood, or one's new sexual feelings.

SEXUAL VALUES

Today's adolescents have much more exposure to sex than teenagers of previous generations. From television to movies, to books, to the Internet, sex acts are performed before their eyes and ears, and sexuality is discussed in both healthy and unhealthy forums. It is natural that they would turn to the church and to God for guidance. It is natural that adolescents connect sexuality with spirituality, as they recognize the new power and vulnerability that is theirs in sexuality. Adolescence is a "teachable moment" for sexuality that the church often neglects.

For the girls I interviewed there still seems to be a large gap between what they are being presented by their parents and in Christian education and what they wish would be addressed. Girls want to discuss sex and sexuality with adults who are not embarrassed; they want to learn about the emotional as well as physical aspects of sex; they want help in making decisions; they wonder why their sexuality is not encouraged and celebrated. They wonder what God thinks of them as sexual beings.

Despite what parents, teachers, and churches have traditionally taught in this culture, sexuality is naturally connected to spirituality. People are embodied spirits—without our bodies we cease to exist as human beings. The Bible connects our bodies with our relationship to God from the beginning chapters of Genesis. The first account of the creation of humans, in Genesis 2, describes them as "formed from the dust of the ground" and given life by God's breath—created as living spiritual bodies. This image of humanity makes it clear, despite a powerful modern mythology, that we are not souls trapped by bodies. Our bodies and spirits together comprise our lives and make us living spiritual beings.

God's original blessing and command for humans, as portrayed in Genesis, had to do with sexuality: "Be fruitful and multiply." The first effect of the "fall" from God's grace in Eden was a recognition of vulnerability as sexual beings: Adam cried to God, who was seeking him in the garden, "I was afraid because I was naked." In our earliest Jewish-Christian myths people are described essentially as bodies alive with God's spirit. God created humans as sexual beings and saw that we were good.

Sadly, even those churches that provide sexuality education for adolescents often "miss the point" as far as the girls are concerned, and avoid the questions the girls are really asking. The following conversation took place with a group of six girls at a large Midwestern church, the week after they had all participated in a sexuality education seminar called CPR (*Creating Positive Relationships*). The conversation began with an acknowledgment that the class was an embarrassment for most students:

> Liz (15): *Our [church] had a thing on CPR and we talked about sex and things like that, but most people were embarrassed about it and they really didn't want to talk about it. But we had this whole lesson. Most of the people really just laughed at it and were very immature about it.*

According to Liz, the problem stemmed from the fact that the teacher was uneasy about teaching sexuality and conveyed this unease to the students. She wonders if she was the only one who thought this ("Am I crazy?"):

I could tell the teacher sort of felt uncomfortable in a way. Or maybe it was just me that felt that way. It just—

Clair (14) interrupts, and expresses her gratitude for any information:

I'm in the eighth grade, and with this CPR thing, I've never heard of this before in my entire life. . . . I never knew any of this, till like this Sunday and last Sunday, and I knew about saving like sex for when you're married. But like nobody ever explained it to me or anything, and I think a lot of the eight graders who are in my class feel the same way. . . . I think it's a really really good thing to talk about, because it just helps you plan your life, basically.

But she acknowledges that the answer to her real question, How do I know what the limits of sexual activity should be at my age, before I'm married? was not answered:

We've asked questions like "How far is too far?" and stuff like that, but our teacher didn't really answer. He just said, you know, "Sex before marriage is wrong," which we all knew that. . . . Well, you know, what do you think about what comes before—like until you can't stop from going on and having sex and stuff? . . . So we really didn't get an answer on that, and I was wondering about that.

Why, she wonders, won't the teacher answer her question?

Why did he try to substitute an easy and well-known answer for a harder one—the real one?

Missy (15) agrees that the subject needs to be discussed because girls her age are not aware that other sexual activities besides intercourse are also wrong:

I believe that we don't talk about the other things that go on, because there's sex and then there's other contacts . . . that are sinful also.

And we don't talk about that. [Girls] are like, "Well, as long as I'm not having sex, I'm okay." But I don't agree with that.

For Missy, girls are the ones who should say no, and they should be aware of what their sexual partners are thinking of them:

. . . because in a guy's eyes sex and those other things are equal. I don't know if you guys believe that or not, but I think if you're doing something that you're not supposed to, it's still a sin. And so I think this is overlooked. And I don't think it's talked about enough in school, and that it's not okay to do that.

When I asked her to be specific about what is sinful and what isn't:

Well, kissing's obviously not [a sin]. I guess, yeah, don't go on beyond a kiss. Removing clothes or going up someone's shirt or something like that. . . . I don't think you should be going beyond a kiss, or whatever.

She begins to hesitate and stumble over words when she hears the rest of the girls disagreeing with her. She thinks maybe she has set the boundary too high. Then, she returns to her original argument, stressing the need for people to be told about all kinds of sexual expression, because knowing that it is wrong might make girls think more (although it might not change their behavior much):

I wish people would know. Because when you think back more, if people actually knew, it would make them stop and think that what they're doing is wrong. And they wouldn't do it. As much.

The girls proceeded to have a heated discussion of when sexuality education should begin. They agreed that girls of all ages need information, but some need more information earlier. They admitted their fears that to teach very specific information at a very young age might seem like encouraging the behavior.

Finally, they settled on an approach that would be tailored more to individual students:

> Missy: *I think that in certain kids, you need it, but others don't. If you're a parent or a youth leader or something, and you think of a kid who might be involved in this kind of stuff, you maybe ought to tell. I don't know. Or you hear from one of their friends, you know. Then you should probably talk to them about it.*

The problem with this approach is that it might embarrass someone by singling her out:

> Heather (16): *But especially in junior high it's hard to separate somebody from the group without pointing a finger at them.*

In private correspondence, the girls shared with me that these concerns were *not* merely abstractions for them. One seventeen-year-old wrote that the last big decision she had made was *to wait six months to kiss [my boyfriend] for the first time.* The last time she had wanted to do something that she felt was wrong was *becoming more physical with my boyfriend than I know we should.* She is worried and unsure about how long she will be able to refrain from "furthering" their activity: *The urge remains. We've only been kissing for two months but the idea of furthering that is in the back of our minds. I know we're strong, but how much and for how long I'm not sure.*

The girls in this church are starving for information on sexuality—even after a two-week seminar devoted to it. They know what their questions are, and they wonder why they weren't answered. They try to formulate their own answers, get discouraged, and give up. They want to make it easier for younger students to get information, but they can't think of ways to provide it without either encouraging "sinful" activity or humiliating them. They worry about their own sexual activity and what it means, and they worry about their friends.

Other girls, in other locations, expressed the same kinds of questions and frustrations. Monica, 19, a college student, struggled with the issue on a different level. She was more sexually experienced than the previous girls; her questions were not "how far?" but rather "in what context?" sexual relationships are appropriate. She wondered, specifically, whether it would be alright to "hook up" (have sexual intimacy) with someone she didn't love, just because she found him attractive and was in the mood for sex: *[I wanted] to hook up with a certain guy when I knew it wouldn't be a really good idea. It's not a relationship type thing. I knew something bad would happen. It just wasn't the right situation. I knew it would end up hurting me, or it might end up hurting him.*

For her, the moral issue was whether someone would be hurt by the experience. Unlike the younger girls, for Monica, morality was not determined by whether the activity was "sinful" in and of itself. Her reference point is relationships; having sex with a guy she was not committed to was wrong because of its effects.

When I asked her what God feels about her sexuality, she responded that God approves, because God created her as a sexual being: *All our temptations and desires and needs for affection and love—God made us that way. So I think that affection, love, physical desires are okay . . . are good, because that's how we were meant to be.* Even in the context of God's approval, however, Monica includes "temptations" as a category—acknowledging that not all acting out of sexual desire is morally right.

Some girls avoided the issue of sexual activity with partners by declining to date at all. Lauren, 18, did not date because of her family's religious beliefs and because she saw what was happening to her friends in relationships with guys. She expressed her thoughts on the subject in very strong terms: *The two strongest values in my life are morality and family, sexual purity and marriage.* For her, sexual purity means no social contact with guys apart from church, school, or work. She feels the temptation (or pressure) to engage in sexual activity might be too great, and she doesn't want to risk compromising her values.

* * *

Many of us who are adults today wished there were places where we could discuss sexuality in relationship to our religious beliefs. Girls today, in a culture that is more sexually explicit but less truthful, less thoughtful, and more exploitative, are in even more desperate need of people and places to go for information and conversation. They want adults to stop talking about sexuality in vague terms; they need us to stop being uncomfortable; they want to know how to formulate sexual values to plan their lives by. The silence of adults regarding appropriate expressions of God-given sexuality for adolescents encourages girls to think in oversimplified all-or-nothing ethical categories. Indeed, when I tell adult church groups that I teach a class on adolescent sexuality, a common all-or-nothing adult response is the half-joking, "What is there to say beyond 'Just say no?'"

Many girls feel that their sexual feelings are not good, because adults won't talk about them; adult silence leads girls to shame, secrecy, guilt, and feelings of being cut off from God. If we don't assist girls to think about sexuality in connection with spirituality, we are complicit with a culture in which sex is mostly portrayed as being about abuse and commercial gain.

Other Questions about Dating

In addition to general questions about sexuality, girls want to talk about how relationships with boys should be experienced and conducted. Some wonder about what kinds of guys they should be dating—if they are Christian, should they only date Christians? Some transform romantic feelings into feelings for God. Some feel pressure to date or be in relationships with boys, even when they don't particularly want to.

Laura is the eighteen-year-old student who has chosen not to date:

Over the last several months there's been a lot going on in my life, especially with guys, which has made it complicated. I just turned 18—

our family values are I'm not supposed to date until I'm 18. Some guys were waiting for me to turn 18 because they liked me. I like them a little bit, but not enough to go out with them or get seriously involved with them. So, I turned 18 this summer and there are several different guys—one down here [at school] and one at home.

Just as her family values about dating protected her from the feeling that she had to date guys she didn't really like, her religious values continue to protect her, even when the family restrictions are gone:

And I was just feeling that I came here to go to school and do what God wants and not really look for any guys or anything. So I'm trying to stay focused on what the Lord wants me to do, and these guys keep bumping into me. God's been answering prayers and just like directing me as far as my relationships.

She is able to trust God and her own instincts about who and when she will date: *When I turn one direction and I'm unhappy or I'm not peaceful, I just say I'm not going there. And I go back the other way and there is peace.*

Monica, a college student, talks about her feelings that she should probably only seriously date guys who share her religious beliefs, but thinks also that it is unrealistic. She wonders if she is right about that:

I don't only date Christian guys, but I think it's a good idea and I think I'm leaning to that direction more and more. . . . It depends on the person and the nature of the relationship. I think ideally it should be a Christian and someone who believes what I believe. But I also think that hasn't happened. I don't know if it's totally wrong not to be with a Christian.

In a move reminiscent of women mystics like Hildegaard of Bingen, some girls transformed the pressure to be in love with boys by talking of "falling in love with Jesus" or being in a "committed relationship with Jesus."

Wendi, an eighteen-year-old from Dallas:

I accepted Jesus into my heart and was baptized in the Holy Spirit when I was three years old. The Holy Spirit filled me more when I was in high school, but these things were just the initial decisions. My important religious experience is walking with Jesus and in him every day. It is learning to fall completely in love with him every day. It is a steady commitment; but it is also a steady communion with my Lord, and this is the greatest "religious" experience I can have because it is not just based on emotion but it is REAL!

Unlike relationships with boys, this relationship is sturdy, consistent ("every day") and is not merely an emotional passing romance—it is "real." She is closer to Jesus than she could ever be with a boy; she walks "with" him and "in him."

Girls' Bodies

At the heart of all questions about sexuality and spirituality is the issue of the meaning of being embodied.

At a time in life when girls' bodies are changing quickly and drastically, girls' feelings about their bodies alternate between pride and humiliation, expectation and fear, love and hate.

Questions about their new bodies and new bodily functions are natural and healthy for early adolescents. Most of the eleven- and twelve-year-olds I interviewed seemed excited about and even protective of themselves and their bodies. In response to questions about their feelings about their bodies, they used words like *special, healthy, valuable, nice, beautiful, well made,* and *neat.* They also felt especially connected to God through their bodies: *My body is special because God made it and I should appreciate it;* and *It is like no other and it was especially created by God.* One eleven-year-old noted that the main requirements for her ideal husband would be that he *respects me and gives me privacy.*

As girls get older, however, a new set of issues about their bodies and their self-images arises. These issues have to do with cultural expectations about being a woman. In her ground-breaking book, *Writing a Woman's Life*, Caroline Heilbrun talks about the intense, but mostly unnamed, pressure for girls and women of the constant feeling of being watched and judged. For Heilbrun, the "watcher" is the male world—which along with womanly behavior (gentleness and nurturing) expects physical perfection. This watching and judging (the "male gaze") establishes men as superior and women (who live under the pressure mostly without protest) as their objects, rather than as subjects, actors, or watchers.[3]

Girls I interviewed experience this pressure of the male gaze as something painful but quite natural to their lives; they submit to it without much thought. Unlike many of the younger girls, the older girls tend to connect their own sense of worth to how well they conform to the physical standard promoted by the male gaze, even though they realize that their selves are much more complex and deep and that the standard is shallow and unattainable. Said Nicole, a fifteen-year-old from Denver:

> Look at what guys our age drool over. They drool over Pamela Anderson Lee, you know. They're like, "Oh, why can't you be like those girls on Baywatch?" In my opinion, I think that guys have to have the finest girl there is, and like be real proud of them, for them—what their perception of it is.

Nicole feels personally ambivalent about following that standard, but she says that she realizes that in order to have a relationship with a boy it is necessary. Her friend, Susanne, agrees with her about most boys. She acknowledges that there are certain boys who don't care what she looks like, with whom she can feel more comfortable. In the end, however, the cultural standard is most important, and those comfortable boys are relegated to the margins:

> There are exceptions—guys that are really nice. There are some guys I wouldn't care if they showed up at my house and I had just woken

up and my hair was in a real mess. And I wouldn't care because they don't care what I look like. But then there are other guys, who, if they showed up at my door, I would want to be at least dressed, and my hair's nice, probably make-up on—"could you come back in an hour?"—so, I don't know—it's like what society expects from you— you have to always look your best.

Nicole observes that the pressure is not on the boys as much as the girls—that girls might be willing to choose boyfriends based on a wider range of attributes than just physical attractiveness:

I think that girls have a tendency to lower their standards a whole lot for guys. I look at some of the girls who are with some of the guys at my school, and it's like those girls must like them for so many other reasons. They must see their personalities. Whereas, for guys at this age, it's only what she wears and how she looks.

At its worst, obsession with the male gaze standard for beauty leads girls to despise themselves. Elizabeth, a seventeen-year-old from Atlanta: *I think my body is a mean joke played upon me by the generations past.* Then, as if shocked by the intensity of her negative feelings toward herself and her genes, she writes: *At least it's healthy. It could have some terrible disease, though, so I shouldn't complain.* She then discounts her feelings or anger and blames them on the fact that she is a teenager: *I am ready to outgrow this adolescent self-hate thing. It is really tedious and a bore.*

The pressure from the male gaze is not limited, however, to the ways in which boys look at them. Girls talked about fierce competitiveness over the ways their bodies looked, and the ways they judge one another's bodies:

Katie, a senior at a boarding school, expresses her ambivalence about her body: *I think my body is fine, but I always can find plenty of things wrong with it. Ultimately, though, it doesn't matter—people come in all shapes and sizes. It's not worth wor-*

rying about. Worrying about it feels like a worthless occupation, because she knows that body diversity is normal.

She can stop worrying when she is away from school, but in presence of her peers, the pressure is too much:

> *I don't know if it's just this school or what, but during the summer most people feel great, and they like the way they look. Then, as soon as they get back here, they start comparing themselves to other people every day. And they do that too much, and it really annoys me, because I don't want the worry or the stress. And you can't help it. It's just human nature. It's just a shame that you have to do it.*

For Katie, competition and stress over the way her body looks are part of human nature, a natural part of life.

* * *

Girls were the most unhappy with themselves and their bodies when their parents were critical of them. Among the girls I interviewed, when one or both parents seemed to join with boys and peers in reinforcing the male gaze standards, it often led to self-destructive feelings and eating disorders.

Marianne, 18, described her body as "a little overweight." She believes this because "of pressure from [her] skinny mother." *My mother implies I'm overweight.* She feels worst about herself when her mother compares their bodies and complains about Marianne's "extra stuff":

> *This past spring break she was really bad about it. We were trying on bathing suits and clothes. My mother is full Chinese, and the Chinese prototype is a flat-chested, flat, skinny legs, very tiny woman. And I've got lots of curves, and so my Mom thinks I'm overweight, because I have extra stuff. This spring break it upset me a lot. Just trying on bathing suits is a big trial—trying on any clothes for any teenager is hell. She goes with me and tries on the same bathing suit, so I could see her and what she looks like in it. Or she'll try on dresses, or she'll see her picture and say, "Oh, I'm too skinny."*

She also has learned to judge her mother's body, perhaps in self-defense:

I think my mother's too skinny. But it's not like she has a problem or diets or anything. She is just skinny to begin with. So I was upset about that.

After her discouraging episode trying on bathing suits with her mother, she returned to school only to have her body criticized by a teacher:

When I came back to school, about a couple weeks ago, I had a run-in with a teacher who also implied that I was . . . I felt like she was implying that I was overweight too. It was a situation where I was trying on clothes for a play.

When she evaluates her own body, she has trouble seeing it realistically with her own eyes. She compares it to other women in her family: *I've got my father's mother's body type. I knew she had big breasts.* Then she evaluates her body in terms of its usefulness in attracting boys—seeing herself through men's eyes: *I guess big breasts are an advantage for an attraction, but I'm getting pretty sick of them.* In her mind, her breasts give her a competitive advantage over other women, but she finds them to be bothersome, even sickening.

The person she most admires is a woman whose body is not tiny like her mother's or her teacher's. *She's my favorite aunt, Sybil—my Mom's sister. She's bigger, and she's just really fun.*

In the worst cases, parents' disapproval of a girl's body can be a factor in dangerous eating disorders. Tammi, 18, is an athlete who tries to follow in her father's track-star footsteps. While attending a boarding school she stopped eating for several months as a part of her training:

I had a lot of trouble in tenth grade. And I stopped eating for a while. I had to tell my parents. I prayed for help to God to tell them, but it didn't help. They just said, "That's ridiculous, you're not thin enough to need help." I didn't talk to my parents for two months last year. They never called me. My fight over food was really a fight over depression.

She had fought battles with her parents over her weight from her early childhood. Her mother had put her on a diet when she was in grade school:

My mom put me on my first diet when I was in second grade. It was absolutely one of the worst things you could ever do to a seven-year-old.

Finally, in the last year, during her sophomore year she had determined to make them proud of her:

Last year I lost about 50 or 60 pounds. And I ran, and I was the second runner on our team. And this year I gained all the weight back, and it just totally destroyed my running career. And that really cut into me, because that was a big thing with my father—my father was a runner—and he lived vicariously through me. When he saw me winning races, and saw me doing extremely well, he got so excited. It was like a way to please my father. So I sort of wasn't doing it for myself, I was doing it for him. So when I stopped winning races and I gained the weight back, I knew my father was really disappointed—it was obvious in his voice. And that was really hard to deal with in the first few calls home.

Although she was eating more normally at the time I interviewed her, she was distressed about losing her father's approval and his pride at her running accomplishments. She is totally conflicted about her eating and her body; she knows what is good for her, but it doesn't bring her the positive attention she craves:

I still can't accept that—I still want to lose weight. But I don't want to be down to 108 pounds, because I didn't get my period for over a year.

Finally, she talks about the ultimate payoff, in her mind, for being thin—her father's shocked and extravagant gaze and praise of her body:

> When I'd lost all that weight, my parents would look at me in a new way. They'd be like, "We're so proud of you." Like I can remember we went out shopping, and I saw this really nice spandex dress, and I was like, "I'm going to go try this on." It shocked them. My father looked at me and said, "Oh my God, you look gorgeous. You have to get that dress."

As she talked, she looked down at her now-healthier body with sadness.

5 ✺

Girls Talk about Violence

My parents never dreamed that a man would one day beat me regularly . . . they'd have been a little less intent on coaxing submissive adolescent behavior from me if they had. Had they known how ugly their church's doctrines could become in the hands of a man willing to use God to justify punching and kicking his pregnant wife, they might even have questioned the church enough that I could have escaped its grasp.

—Hannah Nyala, *Point Last Seen*[1]

I feel God expects me to be nice to everyone, because God cries at violence.

—Sally, 12

Briana was 17, popular, involved in high school activities, and getting ready to graduate and move ahead to college in the fall. Her special talent was singing. She had won awards as a soloist in her school choir and had participated in ensembles that had toured extensively—including a trip to Europe. She also was a featured soloist in her adult church choir. She planned to major in voice at college; it was her favorite way to worship God.

Although her public life seemed charmed, her family life was, in her word, "depressing." The church and her wonderful voice were seeing her through some very hard times at home.

Her father, an alcoholic, had stopped working, and he rarely left the house. He issued commands and threats to her mother—who supported the family with her work at a discount store—and to her sister and her from his torn-up brown recliner in the living room. His major activity, besides drinking, was watching television. But the worst thing about him was that he regularly sexually abused Briana.

Briana's time at home was spent in her bedroom with the door as locked as it could be—it was easily forced open. She never invited friends to visit her house, but she spent hours on the phone talking to them. She read constantly. And she worried about her younger sister. She felt that once she went away to college, her sister would be the next in line for her father's sexual abuse. She had lost many hours of sleep thinking about that probability.

She met with her minister on a Sunday afternoon in May and told him about her home situation and about what had transpired in the previous month. She had begun to have thoughts of killing her father. These thoughts became more and more concrete and urgent. Finally, she had devised and carried out a plan.

Briana and her mother and sister attended church without her father every Sunday morning. She told her minister that several weeks previous on a Sunday morning she followed her plan. She got up before everyone else in the house, retrieved some rat poison from the shed in the back yard, measured out a few tablespoons into a little cup, and carefully poured them into her father's unfinished whiskey bottle from the night before. She shook the bottle vigorously to try to make the poison disappear. Then she left the bottle by his chair where she had found it, and went back to bed until it was time to get ready for church.

Later that morning when she returned home from church she was both relieved and disappointed to find that her father was not dead; he wasn't even sick. He hadn't touched the bottle. She sneaked the poisoned whiskey outside, poured it on the ground, and threw the bottle in the trash can in the garage.

Briana had experienced the violence of her father's emotional tirades daily. She also experienced the horror of his frequent sexual abuse. For a while, she felt totally helpless and vulnerable in the face of it. She did not describe any efforts on the part of her mother to protect her from her father's abuse. Except for the ineffective lock on her bedroom door she had never taken any steps to protect *herself* from her father. But the threat of her father abusing her sister was real enough and horrifying enough to her that she became willing to try to stop him.

Briana was desperate; she felt she had no other alternatives. On that early Sunday morning she couldn't imagine any other course of action. It was no accident that she chose Sunday morning as the time to commit her own act of violence. The church was a place where her gifts were recognized; it was an empowering place for her. In church she was encircled by people who loved her, and she was in the company of her mother and sister—co-victims of her father's abuse. She could commit a horrible act against her father with the knowledge that she would be surrounded by goodness and strength while he died. Sunday morning was the time when her courage was strongest.

It took a tremendous act of strength to break her family's silence about her father; it also took strength to confess her own actions. She trusted her youth minister and hoped he would help her to protect her sister. She felt that God had given her the courage to resist the evil her father was perpetrating on her family, and she believed God would be there with her minister, helping her to find another course of action.

* * *

The violence in Briana's life was overwhelming for her. Sadly, violence—sometimes worse, sometimes less severe—seems to be a normal part of the everyday life of every girl who participated in the study. At the very least, violence is thrust upon girls secondhand in the news broadcasts they hear, the movies they watch, and the books they read. Some have been victims themselves. Almost all who talked about violence knew someone close who had been beaten, sexually abused, robbed, raped, or killed. All live under the threat of violence, which is common to women (and many men) in our culture. The threat of harm or death at the hands of violent people is what many girls said they fear most when they think of the future.

Three main themes emerged in the girls' stories when they spoke of violence: (1) they believe that the world is getting more violent, and that they are in more danger each year; (2) they live in constant awareness of the violence around them, and the effects of violence on their own and others' lives; and (3) they believe victimization is a normal part of life, and expect to experience abuse or violence themselves.

THE WORLD IS A SCARY PLACE

Holly and Anna are 16 and best friends. They spend much of their lives in each other's company, and they were interviewed together. They live in a semi-rural area north of Dallas and attend the consolidated high school. Their families attend the same church. Socially, they date the same boys and spend all of their spare time with a group of about five other girls. Within the first ten minutes of their interview, they brought up the subject of violence. Their main fear is of the gangs in the towns in their area and the threat of being killed if they are in the wrong place at the wrong time. The gangs, they believe, have transplanted themselves into rural Texas after being driven out of the urban centers:

> *All the main gangs are in Dallas, but the police started getting really heavy on patrolling them, and all the gangs went to Gainesville and Sherman. Like the Crips. It's not so bad during the day, but if you go through the wrong part of town . . . it didn't used to be that bad. Now it's like they just kill people for nothing. It's not bad in the part*

of town where we are, but like, if you're in the wrong part of town at night. . . .

They regret that the world has become a place where violence is on everyone's mind all the time. They told a story of being shocked at being mistaken for gang members as they were driving along a road near their movie theater:

The other night, we were going to this little fair thing—it was like a circus—by the mall, and we were going to go over there and watch a movie. We drove by and there was this guy who was bending over and tying his shoes. He looked up and we were driving toward him. We drove around him, but he thought we were trying to run over him, and he got real scared and he started running. We had tinted glass, so he couldn't tell who was in [our car], and he got real scared. And you could tell by looking in his eyes how scared he was—kind of sad, when you have to be scared of someone driving by you.

Violence is so pervasive, even in their rural area, that any unusual action can be taken as a serious threat. The realization that even *they* might be mistaken as potential perpetrators intensified their own awareness of violence, their own fear, and their sadness about the situation.

* * *

Vanesia (15), De Andree (13), and Kim (14) live in urban Dallas. They are also afraid of gangs and other kinds of violence. Vanesia's worst fear for the future is *terrible crime and fighting.* De Andree is afraid and *unhappy because of all the crime that is happening now—just think about the year 2000! As bad as it is now, how much worse will it be when we get older.* She's most afraid of *me dying.* Kim is afraid that *the rate of gang violence and drug using and teen pregnancy, and black-on-black crime will get worse.*

When they are asked if they are anxious about the gangs in their own neighborhood, they respond with mixed feelings. On the one hand, the danger they experience every day from gangs has become commonplace to them. They have acquired knowledge and strategy to try to keep themselves safe. On the other hand, if they think about it too much, they are afraid, even with their strategies for survival.

Vanesia has learned to navigate around gangs. She grew up with many of the kids in the gangs from her neighborhood. She has learned not to interact with them very much, but she tries to stay on friendly terms:

> *I have some friends in a little neighborhood gang, and I know them. I guess I knew most of them before they were in gangs, and I know how they are. And we were like real close. So they don't really scare me. I don't hang around them. I don't go anywhere with them. If I see them in school, it's like, "Hey, what's up? How you doing?"*

But she knows this uneasy casualness is no real protection. She is always conscious of the threat of death:

> *You can't even go outside and play anymore. It's okay, but you still have that fear. . . . It could happen anywhere; you still have that little fear. It's like something is saying you still have a chance of being hurt by anybody—by drive-by . . .*

A voice inside of her is a constant reminder that she could be hurt at any time, anywhere, by anybody. Very few people are totally safe. The kids she grew up with and knows well are the same kids who could hurt her. She could be shot by any carload of people. She is unable to have the unrestrained exuberance of "playing" when she's outside, because she is always on alert—hypervigilant. She's unable to finish her thought; her voice trails off.

She is unhappy that her school has the reputation of being a dangerous place, and she attributes that to the fascination of outsiders with the violence. She says that she has traveled as far away as St. Louis and heard negative comments about her school by people who know it by reputation only:

Anything that happens in my school, it's like publicity and media. Anything can happen. We're well known. Anything that happens at our school, it's always on the radio or on TV.

When Kim is asked if her junior high school is safe she is not able to say for sure:

No—I mean yeah, it's safe enough to go. The schools, they say they're like drug-free and gun-free, but they never know until they're like checking people's lockers all the time. They bring police dogs in, and they start having checks. So they bring dogs in and everything, but they still find them. And that's not really a bad school or a bad neighborhood around there.

Violence and drug searches have become a normal part of her life: she is no longer shocked by events that she knows are disturbing to outsiders. She wishes that drug searches were not necessary, especially in a neighborhood that is considered "safe," and she is angry at the hypocrisy of the schools proclaiming themselves to be drug- and gun-free. She is angry that her peers carry drugs and weapons to school, and she is distressed that police dogs often patrol her school. She wonders who it is that thinks this school is safe enough for her.

* * *

Courtney, 15, goes to public school in Denver. She also has ambivalent feelings about discussing the violence in her school. She admits that she has witnessed violence: *I've seen drive-bys, you know, that kind of thing. I've seen gang fights, but I'm not involved in those things.*

She doesn't want others to dwell on this, however. She takes negative comments about her school as personal insults and thinks (probably correctly) that outsiders talk about her school for reasons that have less to do with danger and more to do with racism and their own prejudices:

I'm really tired of the issue of violence. I was just at my cousin's house the other night, and she's talking about how like "If I went to Washington [High School] I wouldn't want to deal with all the minorities and all this stuff." . . . I [told her], "It's okay, there's so many security guards." And she was like, "Then you shouldn't even be in that school if you have to have security guards."

It's like "Hello!?!"

And it's so obvious that if you see a black man standing at a pay phone with a pager that he must be calling his drug dealer. I'm really tired of hearing that kind of thing. The neighborhood of my school is Black and Hispanic, but the school is very mixed, and there's a lot of different people, and it's a really good school.

She also feels that discussions of violence are often based in adults' bad attitudes toward teenagers in general:

I'm really tired of the attitude that teens today, you know, as a generalized statement, that we're so violent and we're so bad.

In further reflecting on her school, she concedes that she is glad that the authorities make her and her peers aware of the dangers, so that they can take necessary precautions. *It is good that they tell us what's going on, because it makes you so much more aware of the safety issues.* She ends her interview wistfully: *At the same time, if it wasn't going on, you wouldn't have to do these things.*

She has the same implicit question as Kim's: Why is this allowed to go on at my school? Why doesn't someone *do something* about it? Who says this is a safe enough school for me?

VIOLENCE CHANGES EVERYONE'S LIFE

Even if girls have not experienced violence directly, they recognize the effects of violence on others. In addition, they know that they themselves are affected by the violence that has happened to their friends. Sarah, 16, is a sophomore at a private school for girls in suburban Denver.

I go to an all-girls' school, and violence hasn't really affected me that personally. A couple of my good friends have been raped, and that affects them, which affects me.

She resents being segregated from boys at her school and wishes that she was a part of the more rough and tumble world of the public schools in her area. Her school feels too tame for her. She is also very aware that going to a girls' school is not a guarantee that her life will be untouched by violence; two of her good friends at school have been sexually abused. She intuits from their behavior that the rapes have had lasting and detrimental affects on both girls. She can't understand the ways they act, but she attributes what she considers their strange behavior to the lingering effects of violence. The first friend was assaulted in her own bedroom:

The rapist was somebody who just came in her bedroom window, raped her, and then just left. They caught him, but my friend still has flashbacks. Sometimes she'll get so scared that she can hardly move, if something scares her. And I think she plays it up more than she has to, but it still does happen.

This friend exhibits classic signs of post-traumatic stress: hypersensitivity, panic attacks, flashbacks. Sarah doesn't understand these symptoms but accepts that her friend has been deeply affected by living through a rape. She wrestles with whether to believe the intensity of her friend's reactions. Nevertheless, the idea is strongly implanted in her own mind that there is no safe place to hide from violence.

Her second friend, her best friend, was sexually abused when she was a small child. Sarah wisely correlates the friend's current sexual acting out with the early abuse:

My best friend in the whole wide world was raped when she was really little, and I think it really has affected her whole life. She's had sex with so many guys I can't even count them. She doesn't even really remember all of them. One night I just asked her, like, "Name me all the guys you've had sex with." She listed five, and then she was like, "I know I've got some more . . ." And she couldn't remember. Her life's really screwed up . . .

Sarah is incredulous at her friend's sexual activities.

The violence in this girl's life affected her "whole life"—nothing remained untouched. She can't believe that a girl sixteen years old wouldn't be able to remember the names of boys with whom she's had sexual relations. As her best friend, she tries to share her "screwed up" life but has a hard time imagining it or being empathic.

* * *

Crystal, 17, goes to a racially diverse public high school in Boston. She describes how her junior high school was changed in an instant by the shooting of two boys in her seventh grade class:

At my middle school, I guess it was my seventh-grade year, two guys got shot. One of them died, and one of them didn't. And it was really sad. It was like, the guy who died, his name was DW, and in our seventh-grade yearbook there was a whole two or three pages just dedicated to him—a big picture of him on one page. And they got a sculptor to make a sculpture, and it's still at my middle school.

The image of this violence and her friend's victimization remains in her mind, her yearbook, and the courtyard of her school. As she speaks about it, it is clear that she still carries the sadness of her school's loss of innocence and her own grief for her friend.

* * *

Susie, 17, from Atlanta was physically and sexually abused by a former boyfriend. This abuse left her afraid, unable to trust boys, and depressed. She wishes she could erase the relationship from her memory, or at least go back in time and change it.

For her, the relationship was not only painful; it also made her less of a person. If she could change one thing about herself, it would be "to change the destructive relationship" in her past. She wonders how she will rebuild herself.

* * *

Whether the violence was experienced firsthand or through friends, the girls know that it has had lasting effects on everyone it touched. They resent discussions of violence that are covers for racism and general distrust of youth, and they resist disloyalty to their schools. But they rightly are able to connect experiences of violence with extreme fear, sexual acting out, grief, and personal devastation. They understand that an act of violence is an act of destruction. They know that lives can be rebuilt, but not without pain—those affected by violence are changed in their whole lives. Girls wonder why adults don't do more to end violence.

VICTIMIZATION AS NORMAL

Perhaps the most disturbing aspect of talking to girls about violence was hearing their expectation that at some time in their lives they would be victims of violent people. Some of the girls expressed a deep sense of resignation about this, refusing on one level to live in fear and yet believing that part of being a girl and being a teenager is being victimized by others. Girls who have been victims fear that it will happen again. Girls who have not been victims believe that it will probably happen to them.

Courtney, who is tired of discussing violence, believes that statistics show she will be hurt at some point:

> You know, it's not like I'm looking for ways to go get shot. I'm assuming that based on the statistics that something's probably going to happen, but it doesn't bother me; it doesn't really scare me; and I'm really tired of it.

Sarah also feels that she has a good chance of becoming a victim of violence. She is especially concerned about boyfriends:

I've never been, you know, affected directly with any violence. And I know that the chances are that I will be, sometime in my life. I'll have an abusive boyfriend, or whatever. It's not an expectation, but I know that there's a good chance of it happening.

Many girls expressed hopes that their future life partners would respect them, be honest with them, and not hurt them.

* * *

No two girls responded to the pervasive threat of violence in the same way; each girl was affected differently. Some could talk about it; others were less able or willing. The girls who discussed it revealed three different kinds of effects of violence on their lives: (1) Some express feelings of being desensitized to violence—feeling numb about it—not letting themselves feel the full extent of the fear or pain. (2) Most girls will talk about their willingness to protect others from violence, especially their younger siblings or small children. They even suggest that they might use violent means. They do not talk about protecting themselves, however. (3) Many girls wonder why God allows people to be hurt, and they think of the church as an ineffective agent of change.

THE REALITY OF VIOLENCE AND GIRLS' CONSCIOUSNESS

Courtney, who understands the racism inherent in some discussions of violence, talks as if she is so desensitized to it that even the thought of her own victimization doesn't cause her much anxiety.

And I don't know, I think I'm sort of becoming numb to it. Because violence—it's out there, and it does happen, and I'm sure someday

I'll be in the wrong place at the wrong time. But I'm also more aware—it doesn't scare me that much. I mean, it's affected me to the sense that I know it's out there, and I know that I'm going to get hurt sometime, and I'm expecting it.

She discusses violence in an abstract way and claims not to be afraid of the threat that hangs over her. This threat is vivid in her memories of gang fights and drive-by shootings that she has witnessed. She expects to be hurt, and she believes that it will be a matter of bad luck and bad timing ("wrong place at the wrong time"). But the savvy in dealing with her situation that she didn't have when she was younger bolsters her confidence; she's more "aware" and hence, less afraid. She also knows that awareness is not a good enough defense against what's out there. *I know that I'm going to get hurt sometime . . .* Being numb to violence may also be a way of shutting the full impact of its reality out of her consciousness.

Loretta, 18, from New York City answered questions about violence in her life by talking about the death of her friend who had been killed in the previous year by a drunk driver. Loretta talks about not feeling much pain, although she loved her friend. She attempts to find meaning in the death, and is consoled that it taught many of her peers about their own finitude and their own vulnerability to being harmed:

I looked at her death more as . . . a lot of good things happened with that. . . . It helped a lot of us to understand that we weren't invincible. Especially when you're sixteen, seventeen, eighteen . . . you really have that belief that you're invincible, that you can do anything, and nothing will harm you.

Loretta talks about the circumstances of her friend's death, and her feeling that the death was not a tragedy, because of the way her friend had lived:

She was happy, and she lived a life she wanted to live. Yes, it's hard any time someone that young dies, but I didn't think of it as if it was a tragedy . . . so much as it was time. . . . I mean, I loved her and she was a really good friend to a lot of different people, so it was sort of as though she had made her mark. It wasn't as though she had died not doing anything, or not touching anyone, so it made it a little different.

Along with Courtney, Loretta expresses a kind of resignation about violence: "it was time" for her friend to die—a matter of fate. The grief and shock one would expect to hear from a close friend of a girl killed by a drunk driver were not present. She tried to write a happy ending for her friend as a person who was loved, had made "her mark," and had touched others. These words were not disingenuous, but they were not heartfelt or spoken with passion. Loretta was "numb" to the reality of her loss but also grateful that through her friend's death she was made more aware of her own vulnerability to being harmed.

* * *

Loretta, Courtney, and Vanesia have different strategies for dealing with the persistent presence of violence in their lives. Loretta recognizes the value of being aware of danger, but remains numb to her present reality: the loss of her beloved friend to a violent driver. She has a sense that fate and timing are more important factors in becoming a victim of violence than anything else. The important thing for her is to have lived a life that "made a mark." Courtney also moves from awareness to numbness and back. Her awareness makes her more safe and less afraid, but she seems to believe, like Loretta, that safety is in the end a matter of luck and timing. Vanesia hears a voice telling her to be afraid all the time. This voice inhibits her from ever really enjoying her life—the danger could come at any time, from any source.

PROTECTING OTHERS IS BETTER THAN PROTECTING OURSELVES

Girls who talk about being victimized by violence as a normal part of their own lives do not believe that it should be a normal part of the lives of others. While they rarely express willingness or preparedness to defend themselves from violence, many talk as if they would be willing to go as far as killing to protect other innocent victims, especially children.

Holly, who lives in rural Texas, says that her ambition for her future life includes taking care of those who can't care for themselves. Part of that mission is to help rid the world of those who would hurt the vulnerable: *I'd like to take care of all the good people, and kill all the bad people.*

When her friend, Anna, expresses shock at Holly's fierce words, she begins to apologize: *It's not very nice, but . . . little kids can't even play outside. It's bad. It's worse now than it was when we were little.* Her willingness to "kill" is predicated on her understanding that the world has degenerated to a place where little children can no longer be safe doing something as normal as playing outside. In her mind, the deterioration of the quality of these children's lives causes her to feel fierce anger that transcends even the niceness code.

De Andree, from urban Dallas, thinks that adults and "kids" should join together to make the situation better for the children who will be coming after her: *We all need to work together to make sure the world will be better for kids who will be our age.* She doesn't appear to feel that work should be done to make things better for *herself*. The danger that she and her friends confront does not seem compelling enough to her to involve others in eradicating it. The "kids who will be our age" in the future deserve better than she does.

Sometimes girls are willing to protect themselves only if others are also threatened. Elizabeth, 19, from Philadelphia, had been having trouble for a year with an ex-boyfriend and a friend of his who continually harassed and threatened her.

Elizabeth had apparently lived in silence with the situation throughout the year. Finally, however, the situation hit a turning point for her when the ex-boyfriend began harassing her current boyfriend: . . . *then their attention was turned to my current boyfriend. When they attacked him, I finally wrote back a nasty letter, defending myself and chastising the two of them.*

Only when her current boyfriend began to be "attacked" did she feel strongly enough about the situation to begin to defend herself—by writing a retaliatory letter. She chastised her tormentors only as part of a response to their mistreatment of someone else.

Elizabeth's resolve to defend herself did not last long, however. She characterizes her letter to them as "nasty"—a strong negative in her mind. She regrets and feels guilty about writing it—believing that through it she had sunk to greater depths than her harassers: *I stooped to their level and lower and still feel guilty for it.*

WHY DO GOD AND THE CHURCH ALLOW VIOLENCE TO CONTINUE?

Girls who have experienced violence often have a more difficult time relating to God and the church. Beliefs about God change, or God begins to fade from their immediate concern. Sometimes they try not to think about religion, because they can't reconcile the violence they have seen with their images of a God who loves them and the world.

Maria, 18, is the secretary of her church, an ethnically diverse congregation in West Dallas. Three years previously she had been a member of the youth advisory team and president of her youth group when one of her good friends was shot and killed. She talks about the shooting:

One of my friends, one of the members of the youth group, was murdered about three years ago . . . Tim. He was shot. He was the vice-president of the youth group and in charge with me. He was in a house and they broke in, and they shot him point blank, so—there was no struggle or anything.

Eric's death was her first real experience of loss due to violence, and it shattered her belief that the world is a safe place. The morals and values her mother instilled in her didn't protect her from losing a friend:

I've always been and I still am kind of sheltered from everything. My mother is so strict with me, and she's brought me up with morals, and values, and things, and I've always been sheltered from violence and things that are going on. So it was a shock and kind of hard to handle, because that has been the only time I've had to deal with losing a close friend.

In the aftermath of the murder, she felt close to God and alienated from God at the same time:

In this situation I felt closest to God and distant from him. I think this situation kind of pulled me away from him, but at the same time it made me feel close. I felt closest to God, because I feel that he got me through it. Without him I don't think I would have, and it was also with friends and family that supported me. But at the same time I felt distant from him, because that's the time that I started questioning him and doubting him, and you know, wondering, "Why me?" or "Why my friend?" So it goes both ways, me feeling close to him and me feeling distant.

Maria continues to attend church and to participate in national youth events in her denomination, but God is not currently an important part of Maria's life. Between the time of the murder and my interview with her, God had become more and more distant.

I'm in this stage, kind of, right now where I feel kind of distant from God. Religion hasn't been that important, hasn't been up there in a long time.

Her problem with God stems from Tim's death and from her realization that violence and cruelty are pervasive in her world:

I think I kind of don't understand why, if he is such a powerful God, I don't understand why we have so much crime and so much death and things like that. There's so much cruelty in the world, and it seems like things are just getting worse. They're not getting any better and, I think, I don't understand. If he's supposed to be so loving and powerful, then why are so many things going on? So I think that's the only thing I have with God.

She has repeatedly asked adults in the church, including her ministers, to answer her questions. She is not satisfied with any of the explanations given, and is not willing to forget the questions in order to restore a closer relationship with God:

It's been explained to me so many times why things like this happen. But I still kind of have doubts. I don't think it's going to get any better unless someone changes it.

It's up to "someone" to change the world. She has doubts that God will be much use in the process.

* * *

Krystal, a native of New York City, has another theory of violent behavior and who is responsible. She doesn't believe that it is God's responsibility to prevent violence directly. Nevertheless, her perception of God has changed as acquaintances have been killed:

I know acquaintances more than friends who've been killed through violence, and I think that some of them have changed my perception of God. I began to wonder how you can allow anyone to stay in the position to be in violent states. Because I think a lot of the violence that transpires, at least between young people, comes from a lack of education and a lack of things to do. And I'd like to believe that there are a lot of ways to fix that.

In her mind young people take part in violence when they lack education and/or are bored. The solution to violence involves changing the environment of those youth. She wonders why God doesn't inspire leaders or others to change a situation for young people that is so conducive to violence.

> For those ways [to fix the situation] not to occur, that sort of changes my perception of God—how God can allow, whether it be legislature or people in general, those acts to perpetuate. I'm from New York, so on the nightly news we hear about little kids in crossfires and stuff. And I think that God should . . . especially since I live in a large city, and a lot of the crime we see has a lot to do with drugs . . . I wonder . . . how anyone can allow children to die like that.

In the end, she finds it hard to talk about. She hesitates, and her voice drifts off. The government, "people in general," and God all seem to be responsible for allowing children to die.

She is left puzzled.

* * *

Kim, De Andree, and Vanesia do not have questions about God's justice. They are more concerned with the church, and frustrated that the church has done little to change the dangerous situations in their neighborhoods and at school.

Kim is frustrated that the church seems to be more concerned with its own peace than her safety: *The church could do something about it, but they're scared.*

De Andree believes that God is furious with the perpetrators of violence and with the church. God is also, in her view, shamed by the pervasiveness of violence. She wants to encourage "everybody" to take part in working to change their neighborhoods.

> God does not like this—is probably very angry—angry at everybody. I'm serious!! He feels disgraced by it. And everybody would have to suffer just because of some people. Everybody needs to work together.

When asked if the church helps them to stay out of trouble, they respond with giggles and exaggerated wide eyes. Their community leaders have obviously let them know that gangs, drugs, and other kinds of violence are not acceptable: *They just put fear in us so we will know not to do something like that. It would be all over.*

The church can help them to stay beyond the reach of perpetrators of violence by encouraging them and standing by them as they resist the temptation to join in. It also provides activities for them to "keep them off the streets." They believe, however, that the church will not fight to reduce the influence of gangs and violent people in the community, because it is afraid to be involved. They are grateful for any help they can get in their struggles with violence—grateful that the church is a safe place for them—but they are frustrated and confused about the church's unwillingness to take on the real battle.

* * *

For Maria, Krystal, Kim, Vanesia, and De Andree, God, adults, and the church are disappointments. They see the reality and pervasiveness of violence in their communities clearly. From their perspective adults are failing them in two ways: (1) by hypocritically denying the extent of the violence and (2) by failing to "work together" to solve the problem. They are hesitant to talk about God; but when they do, it is clear that they are disappointed with God also. *If he's supposed to be so loving and powerful, then why are so many things going on? I wonder . . . how anyone can allow children to die like that.*

The explanations adults give them don't make sense, and they admit that they are prone to doubts about God's power and love. They believe that most adults are not able to appreciate the ways that violence makes them struggle—even with the deepest questions of the Christian faith.

* * *

What does pervasive violence mean to girls? One college student I interviewed in Philadelphia told me that *the worst part of being a girl is being afraid to walk alone at night.* Violence adds fear and unnecessary limits to girls' lives. They can't walk at night, play outside, go to school, drive to neighboring towns, or even sleep in their bedrooms at night without voices in the backs of their minds telling them to be watchful. Violence disturbs relationships. Friends act strangely out of post-traumatic stress symptoms. New boyfriends need to be protected from old. Violence makes them lie awake at night worrying about younger siblings. Violence can tempt them to act violently themselves.

Parents and churches are challenged in two important ways by these girls. First, reflection on theologies that stress suffering and martyrdom is in order. Girls seem to believe that those they love should not have to suffer violence, and they talk about being willing to champion others against violent people. They do not talk about championing themselves, however. They seem to believe that, somehow, *they* should be able to "handle it." They expect no one to protect them. To the extent that they themselves have suffered violence, they understand it as normal suffering. Those who haven't been victimized talk about feeling resigned that they will be victims someday.

The church is participating in the victimization of girls to the extent that their acceptance of violence is rooted in theologies that accept suffering as normative, or even admirable. Where are theologies that teach girls expectations of being safe, or the goodness of self-protection? As Carol Adams writes:

> When a [girl] wonders where God [is] in her suffering, we need to remind her that she has been forced to ask this question because her community deserted her. Her theological constriction arises because we have allowed . . . her trauma to be ever-present, rather than being able to secure it in the past.[2]

Nurturing Girls' Spirituality

Spirituality, for girls, is about relationships. It is especially about girls' relationships with God. God is the one who protects them in time of trouble, who cherishes them even when they "mess up," who nurtures and shelters just like a tree does, who "cries at violence," and who helps them stay in healthy relationship with others. God is the stable point in their changing worlds.

In order to be able hear girls at the level necessary for meaningful interaction with them, adults need first to listen to themselves and to remember their own lives as adolescents. The goal of this book, and of the study out of which it grew, is to introduce adults—women and men—to girls as spiritual people. As has been shown, this is often a difficult task. Girls have been taught to be nice: silent and mistrustful of their own voices and feelings. They have been taught to defer to adults and other authorities, and to keep their own most important thoughts and feelings "underground." Sometimes their thoughts and feelings are so far underground that even the girls lose touch with them.

The girls whose voices are presented here represent girls from many different kinds of backgrounds. Girls from inner cities, girls from the suburbs, girls from small rural towns, girls who are members of families with substantial economic means, and girls whose families live close to poverty are present here. African American, Asian, Latina, and Anglo girls are present. Girls who are close to being young adults, and girls who are barely adolescent are here. Girls who are Protestant, Episcopalian, Roman Catholic, and self-proclaimed atheists speak here.

These girls have different concerns and different feelings about topics of concern to all. They represent differing levels of maturity. Yet, there are common themes: For the most part the girls who spoke with me love their families. They love their church communities, although there are aspects of church that confuse them and anger them. They respect their church leaders and are hungry for guidance from them; they are especially grateful for women who take the time to get to know them and to share their wisdom.

Most girls appreciate the chance to take part in worship services and to contribute their gifts to the church. Many wish worship was different, addressing more of their concerns. They resent adults who try to speak for them or to tell them what they must believe. They wish and hope that the church will become stronger in its protection of them from the violence of their "outside" worlds. They wonder why church leaders often seem to avoid answering hard questions; many feel adults don't understand their lives well, or don't take them seriously.

This project hopes to encourage women and men who are in positions of responsibility for girls to listen to and for girls' spiritual voices. Girls need adults who will listen to them and affirm them even when their questions and actions aren't stereotypically nice. Girls voices are the voices of fresh understanding and new uncynical confrontations with the most raw and most troubling aspects of faith. Girls who are able to move beyond niceness will often articulate remarkably uncomfortable insights and challenges. If we listen well, they will call us back to our own questions, and especially make us reconfront the ones we'd covered over or left behind unanswered. Real listening means allowing ourselves to be questioned at very deep levels. It will force us to reconsider our own spiritualities, and may challenge us to reevaluate the credibility of our beliefs and the integrity of our actions in the religious realm.

To the contrary, not listening means teaching girls the false and harmful "lessons" that many of us learned when our own questions were not heard: that our relationship with God can't bear the weight of real scrutiny; that the church isn't the proper place for doubts; that real and intense feelings such as pain and anger and joy and gratitude are not appropriate for the community of faith.

Families and faith communities that recognize the challenge of nurturing girls' voices and participating in their developing relationships with God may hope to enjoy the benefits of spiritually strong young women. These young women will be better able to resist the cultural message that their voices, lives, bodies, and feelings aren't important. They will be encouraged to keep their questions, challenges, and dreams alive. They will learn to live and thrive in relationships with God, to whom they bring their deepest questions, doubts, and concerns, and from whom they derive strength and purpose.

Communities of faith need to equip themselves to listen to and to learn from girls. Only if they listen, can they protect girls and nurture girls' resistance to cultural oppression and evil. Only communities that take girls seriously can assist them in moving beyond the cultural ideal of niceness to develop healthier, more intimate, more mature and empowering relationships with their peers, their families, and with other adults. Only adults and communities that listen carefully, with engaged hearts, minds, souls, and spiritualities can assist girls in developing their own real and saving relationships with God.

Notes

Preface

1. "A Cultural Model of Perfection for Adolescent Girls," from Lyn Mikel Brown and Carol Gilligan, *Meeting at the Crossroads: Women's Psychology and Girl's Development* (Cambridge: Harvard Univ. Press, 1992), 61.

Introduction

1. See Erik Erikson, *Young Man Luther* (New York: W. W. Norton, 1958) 118–19.

2. See Erik Erikson, *Identity, Youth, and Crisis* (New York: W. W. Norton, 1968). See also Lyn Mikel Brown and Carol Gilligan, *Meeting at the Crossroads: Women's Psychology and Girls' Development* (Cambridge, Mass.: Harvard Univ. Press, 1992); Carol Gilligan, Nona P. Lyons, and Trudy J. Hanmer, eds., *Making Connections: The Relational Worlds of Adolescent Girls at Emma Willard School* (Cambridge, Mass.: Harvard Univ. Press, 1990).

3. See, for example, American Association of University Women, *Hostile Hallways: The AAUW Survey on Sexual Harassment in America's Schools* (Washington, D.C.: AAUW Educational Foundation, 1993); *How School Shortchanges Girls* (Washington, D.C.: American Association of University Women Foundation and National Education Association, 1992); Barrie Levy, *Dating Violence: Young Women and Danger* (Seattle: Seal Press, 1991); Myra and David Sadker, *Failing at Fairness: How America's Schools Cheat Girls* (New York: Charles Scribner's Sons, 1994).

4. A recent study on boys, "Listening to Boys' Voices," sponsored by Harvard Medical School, indicates that boys are at comparable risk during their preschool years when they are first inculcated into the "Boy Code,"

which proscribes for them such things as emotional vulnerability, closeness, and gentleness. See William Pollack, *Real Boys: Rescuing Our Sons from the Myths of Boyhood* (New York: Random House, 1997).

5. Feminist social-scientific research stresses not only listening to women's voices but also analyzing the ways in which the voices have been affected by the broader social structure in which women live. It is important to listen carefully and also to understand culturally the voices one hears. See M. L. DeVault, "Talking and Listening from Women's Standpoint: Feminist Strategies for Interviewing and Analysis," *Social Problems* 37/1 (1990): 96–116.

6. For information on qualitative research methodology see: Steven J. Taylor and Robert Bogdan, *Introduction to Qualitative Research Methods,* 3d ed. (New York: John Wiley & Sons, Inc., 1998); and L. Bickman and D. J. Rog, *Handbook of Applied Social Research Methods* (Thousand Oaks, Calif.: Sage, 1998).

Chapter 1

1. Barry Lopez, *Crow and Weasel* (New York: Harper Collins, 1993), 60.

2. Carol Gilligan, Nona P. Lyons, and Trudy J. Hanmer, eds., *Making Connections: The Relational Worlds of Adolescent Girls at Emma Willard School* (Cambridge, Mass.: Harvard Univ. Press, 1990).

3. See, for example, V. C. Andrews, *Darkest Hour* (New York: Pocket Books, 1993); *Hidden Jewel* (New York: Pocket Books, 1995).

4. See, for example, Latoya Hunter, *The Diary of Latoya Hunter: My First Year in Junior High School* (New York: Crown Publishers, 1992); and Anne Frank, *Anne Frank: The Diary of a Young Girl*, ed. Otto H. Frank and Mirjam Pressler, trans. by Susan Mossotty (New York: Doubleday, 1995).

5. See, for example, Peggy Ornstein, *Schoolgirls* (New York: Doubleday, 1994); and Mary Pipher, *Reviving Ophelia: Saving the Selves of Adolescent Girls* (New York: Ballantine Books, 1994).

6. Peggy Ornstein, *Schoolgirls*, citing the American Association of University Women, *Hostile Hallways: The AAUW Survey on Sexual Harassment in America's Schools* (Washington, D.C.: AAUW Educational Foundation, 1993), 5.

7. Pipher, *Reviving Ophelia,* 39.

8. Latoya Hunter, *The Diary of Latoya Hunter: My First Year in Junior High School* (New York: Crown, 1992) 25.

9. Gilligan et al., *Making Connections*, 14.

10. Except for two of the girls whom I had known since they were small children, I was a stranger to all the girls I interviewed.

Chapter 2

1 David Finkelhor, *Childhood Sexual Abuse* (New York: The Free Press, 1984); Gail Wyatt, "The Sexual Abuse of Afro-American and White Women in Childhood," *Child Abuse and Neglect* 9 (1985): 507–19.

2. Diana Russell, *The Secret Trauma* (New York: Basic Books, 1986).

3. U.S. Department of Justice, *National Crime Victimization Survey, 1992–1993*, "Female Rape Rates, by Race and Age of Victim, 1993."

4. Federal Bureau of Investigation, *Supplementary Homicide Report*, 1992.

5. Carol Gilligan, "Teaching Shakespeare's Sister: Notes from the Underground of Female Adolescence," in Carol Gilligan, Nona P. Lyons, and Trudy J. Hanmer, eds., *Making Connections: The Relational Worlds of Adolescent Girls at Emma Willard School* (Cambridge, Mass.: Harvard Univ. Press, 1990), 6–27.

6. A few recent titles include *Chamber of Fear* (New York: Golden Books, 1998); *Cheerleaders: The New Evil* (New York: Pocket Books, 1994); *The Hitchhiker* (New York: Scholastic Books, 1993); *Scream* (New York: Golden Books, 1998); and *Forbidden Secrets* (New York: Pocket Books, 1996).

7. Recent titles include: *Darkest Hour* (New York: Pocket Books, 1993); *Hidden Jewel* (New York: Pocket Books, 1995).

8. Melvin Burgess, *Smack* (New York: Holt, 1998).

9. Robert Cormier, *Tenderness* (New York: Delacorte, 1997).

10. Brock Cole, *The Facts Speak for Themselves* (Arden, N.C.: Front Street, 1997).

11. Norma Fox Mazer, *When She Was Good* (New York: Arthur A. Levine, 1997).

12. Sara Mosle, "The Outlook's Bleak," *New York Times Magazine*, August 2, 1998, 34, 36; Alison Lurie, "Reading at Escape Velocity," *New York Times Book Review,* May 17, 1998.

13. Jennifer M. Brown and Cindi Di Marzo, "Why So Grim?" *Publishers Weekly*, February 16, 1998, 120–23.

14. Mark Edmundson, *Nightmare on Main Street: Angels, Sadomasochism, and the Culture of Gothic* (Cambridge, Mass.: Harvard Univ. Press, 1997).

15. Ibid., 5.

16. Ibid., 67.

17. Ibid., 75.

18. Robert Kegan, *The Evolving Self: Problems and Process in Human Development* (Cambridge, Mass.: Harvard Univ. Press, 1982), 147.

Chapter 3

1. For further reading see Erik Erikson, *Young Man Luther* (New York: W. W. Norton, 1958); and *Identity, Youth, and Crisis* (New York: W. W. Norton, 1968); Carol Gilligan, *In a Different Voice: Psychological Theory and Women's Development* (Cambridge, Mass.: Harvard Univ. Press, 1982); Carol Gilligan, Nona P. Lyons, and Trudy J. Hanmer, eds., *Making Connections: The Relational Worlds of Adolescent Girls at Emma Willard School* (Cambridge, Mass.: Harvard Univ. Press, 1990); Lyn Mikel Brown and Carol Gilligan, *Meeting at the Crossroads: Women's Psychology and Girls' Development* (Cambridge, Mass.: Harvard Univ. Press, 1992); Judith V. Jordan et al., *Women's growth in connection : writings from the Stone Center* (New York: Guilford, 1991).

2. Erik Erikson, *Identity, Youth, and Crisis*, 87.

3. Carol Lakey Hess, *Caretakers of Our Common House* (Nashville: Abingdon, 1997), 145–50.

4. Erik Erikson, *Identity, Youth, and Crisis*, 159.

5. The negative feelings of Roman Catholic girls in this study mirror the feelings of feminist women who are members of the Roman Catholic Church. A study of feminist women and the church found that four out of five Roman Catholic women who participated often feel intensely alienated from the church. According to this study, more women feel alienated in the Catholic church than in any other denomination. Miriam Therese Winter, Adair Lummis, and Allison Stokes, *Defecting in Place: Women Claiming Responsibility for Their Own Spiritual Lives* (New York: Crossroad, 1994), 101.

6. James W. Fowler, *Stages of Faith* (San Francisco: Harper Collins, 1981), 151–73.

7. Sharon Parks, *The Critical Years* (San Francisco: Harper & Row, 1986).

Chapter 4

1. Joan Jacobs Brumberg, *The Body Project: An Intimate History of American Girls* (New York: Random House, 1997), 48.

2. Naomi Wolf, *Promiscuities: The Secret Struggle for Womanhood* (New York: Random House, 1997), xxv.

3. Caroline Heilbrun, *Writing a Woman's Life* (New York: Ballantine Books, 1988), 82–83.

Chapter 5

1. Hannah Nyala, *Point Last Seen: A Woman Tracker's Story* (Boston: Beacon Press, 1997).

2. Carol Adams, *Woman Battering* (Minneapolis: Fortress Press, 1994), 113.

Index

niceness, ix–xi, 18, 20, 111, 119–120
Nyala, Hannah, 97, 127n. 1
Ornstein, Peggy, 124nn. 5, 6
overweight, 93
parents
    criticism from, 93–94
    living through girls, 95
Parks, Sharon, 64, 126n. 7
pastors
    separation from, 56
    women, 53–54
peers, disagreement with, 71–72
Pipher, Mary, 18, 124nn. 5, 7
Pollack, William, 124n. 4
prayer, 31
premarital sex, 76, 85–88, 105–6
Pressler, Mirjam, 124n. 4
psychological development, 3
punishment (by God), 33
questioning, 4, 14, 67, 84, 86, 114
racism, 103–4, 108
rape, 105
relationships, 3, 9, 107–8
    destructive, 107–8
religion, girls' choice, 74–77
religious values, 89
Rice, Anne, 27
risk-taking
    dangerous behavior, 4
    vulnerability within group, 73
Rog, D. J., 124n. 6
role models, girls need for, x, 53, 55–57, 77
Russell, Diana, 125n. 2
sacraments, 37, 59–60
Sadker, David, 123n. 3
Sadker, Myra, 123n. 3
salvation, 15, 33

sermons, girls disconnected, 59, 76
sermons, women's roles, 58
sex, multiple partners, 105–6
sexual abuse, 17, 98, 105
sexual purity, 87
sexuality
    church teaching , 82–83
    and commitment, 87
    experimentation, 81, 86
    information sources, 81–82, 84–86
    moral aspects, 85–88
    spiritual aspects, 82–83, 87
society, attitude towards teens, 104
spirituality, ix–xi, 3, 59, 119
    adolescent, 11, 17–18
St. Ignatius Loyola, 31
stereotyping, 104, 120
Stine, R. L., 27
Stokes, Allison, 126n. 5
suffering, as theological norm, 117
Taylor, S. J., 124n. 6
testing (by God), 33
trust, 51, 53
victimization, 26, 107–8, 111
violence
    boyfriends, 108, 110, 111
    church's response, 115–17
    numbness to, 108, 110
    in schools, 103, 106
    self-protection, 112, 117
    theological aspects, 117
Winter, Miriam Therese, 126n. 5
Wolf, Naomi, 81, 126n. 2
women, and subordinate roles, 22
women's roles, 58, 76
worship, 51, 57, 58, 60–63
Wyatt, Gail, 125n. 1
youth services, 60–63